Taking the Lead

Taking the Lead

A Dog at Number 10

John Crace

CONSTABLE

CONSTABLE

First published in Great Britain in 2024 by Constable

5 7 9 10 8 6

A CIP catalogue record for this book
is available from the British Library.

ISBN: 978-1-40872-127-8

Typeset in Sabon LT by Hewer Text UK Ltd, Edinburgh
Printed and bound in Great Britain by Clays Ltd, Elcograf S.p.A.

Papers used by Constable are from well-managed
forests and other responsible sources.

MIX
Paper | Supporting responsible forestry
FSC® C104740

Constable
An imprint of
Little, Brown Book Group
Carmelite House
50 Victoria Embankment
London EC4Y 0DZ

The authorised representative
in the EEA is
Hachette Ireland
8 Castlecourt Centre
Dublin 15, D15 XTP3, Ireland
(email: info@hbgi.ie)

An Hachette UK Company
www.hachette.co.uk

www.littlebrown.co.uk

To Pitt Lim and all the cardio and A&E staff at St George's Hospital. I owe you.

Contents

Chapter 1

Forgive me. Neither my hearing nor my eyesight are quite what they used to be. Long walks leave me slightly breathless these days. As I once said to Leonard Cohen, I ache in the places where I used to play. In the past, after completing one circuit of the common, I used to nag to go round again. Now I'm more than happy to slope off home. Most mornings, I go upstairs for a lie-down on the bed. To keep an eye on the back garden. To watch the parakeets fighting over the fruit in the crab apple tree. A dog can waste hours doing that. Though mostly I just like to doze. I do a lot of sleeping these days.

The years seem to roll round a lot faster than they used to. When I was young, the seasons felt endless. More smells than I knew what to do with. They used to drive me crazy. Time had no real meaning. I just lived in the present. Now, I feel more conscious of every passing moment. Things somehow matter both

far more than they used to and far less. I can feel the days ticking by. Making fun of my attempts to slow time down. To turn each hour into a day.

I'm now twelve and a half years old. That half is significant when you're a dog. At a very rough calculation, one human year is the equivalent to seven dog years. Though time isn't quite that linear. We mutts compress a lot of our ageing into the early years of our life. By the time we are a year old, we are more or less grown up. Physically, at any rate.

But this is by the by. What matters is that I am now an old dog. Probably somewhere in my eighties. Time is not on my side. If I'm very lucky, I guess I could be around for another four years. I certainly do my best to keep fit. I keep count of my daily steps and pack in the strength training in the gym. But when your time's up, there's little you can do but go gracefully. Try not to moan too much about life being unfair. What I'm really saying is that this time next year I might not be here.

Humans say that dogs have no concept of death. That we exist only in the present. We're here until we're not. That somehow this makes us zen. Well, that's rubbish. Of course we think about death. How could we not? We aren't that stupid. Think about it. Even as a young dog, we confront our mortality. When I was a puppy, I would frequently meet the same dogs and humans out on Tooting Bec Common. Then, you think you will live forever. But over the years, you stop seeing the same faces. Sometimes, you see the humans out with a different dog. A younger dog. And gradually you hear whispers. Piece things together. You come to understand the finite nature of existence.

Once, I even got the chance to say goodbye. I was out taking one of my humans for a walk and I bumped into Elsie, a dachshund I had known for about seven years. She seemed to be distracted, dawdling more than usual. So I asked if she was OK. 'Not really,' she said. 'I've got cancer. Inoperable. And I'm in a fair bit of pain. So we're going to the vet later this afternoon to have me put down. But first we're doing my favourite walk for one last time. So I can take in the smells and the sounds. Memories to take with me for whatever comes next.' It was a touching encounter. I've never forgotten Elsie.

I haven't reached that moment. But I am at the stage where I do increasingly think of death. Not that I believe in an afterlife. I don't think I am headed for a doggy heaven where I can be reunited with my brothers and sisters. Or where my humans give me endless cuddles. I just think you're in a state of not being. The world carried on happily without me for billions of years before I was born and I dare say it will go on for billions more years when I've died. Assuming that Rishi Sunak and Therese Coffey haven't managed to destroy the planet.

Don't get me wrong. I'm not about to offer myself up to Dignitas just yet. Only last week I injured my front leg and I could hear John, my male human, saying. 'I think he's had a stroke. He doesn't seem to know where he is.' I had to take emergency evasive action. 'Look, you moron,' I snapped. 'I've just pulled a muscle. There's nothing wrong with me. There's no way you're going to put me in the car and have me put down.' Thank God, the message finally got through.

But I am almost ready to die. When the time comes. I've had a good life. An interesting life. In many ways my work is done. I've taught my humans how to love. No dog can do more. That's our gift to the world. It's the first thing we learn in dog school. But it's also time to tell my story. To bear witness to the chaos of the past twelve years. One of the most surreal periods in British history. There are very few of us dogs around who have lived through six prime ministers. I've done more than that. I've even met them all. Advised them. Not that they took any notice. I even kept all my WhatsApp messages. Which is more than Boris Johnson and Rishi did.

More than that, I can remember what it was like to live in Britain before Brexit. When not every schnauzer got told to go back home by XL bullies. I was also personal friends with some of the late queen's corgis. So I happened to be at Balmoral on the day she died. For years, people have been begging me to write my autobiography. To tell people what really went on inside government. I can remain silent no more.

Chapter 2

How rude of me. I should have introduced myself. My full name is Herbert Hound. Though most people call me Herbie. Or Herbs.

Actually, it's a little more complicated than that. Because my real name is Eric. That's what my mother called me. But no one told my humans that when I adopted them. To them, I was nameless. It didn't even occur to them to ask what my mother and siblings called me. They just assumed I'd never had a life before them. So, Herbie I became. I can't say I mind that much now. Life's too short to carry on fighting those sorts of battles you're never going to win. But when I'm feeling low, I can still hear my mother's voice. 'Come along now, Eric. Stop dawdling.'

I was born on 17 September 2011. A Saturday, I think. There were six of us puppies. Ian, Jeff, Stanley, Sophie, Lizzie and me, Eric. And my mum, Hattie. I never knew my dad. He didn't even drop by once to

say hello. I still find that odd. If I had ever been a father, I'm sure I would have been curious to meet my children. But not him. I guess he was old-school. Dogs weren't very woke when I was young. Nobody gave their feelings a second thought. Especially if you were a bloke.

All I do know about my father I got from my mum and even she was fairly hazy on the details. His name was Brian and he was a black-and-white cocker spaniel who had a bit of a reputation in the neighbourhood for being a flirt. 'He was very handsome,' my mother said. 'I knew it was a bad idea to get off with him. That he wasn't interested in long-term relationships. But I just couldn't say no to him. We only slept together one time and then I never saw him again.'

This technically means I come from a broken home. Though that would rather suggest I ever had a home to be broken. I spent my early days in either a cardboard box or a cage. I'm not trying to give you a hard-luck story. This is just the way it was. For ages, I used to fantasise about Brian. Was he really that feckless? If we bumped into one another in the street, would we even recognise each other? Did he feel guilty for having abandoned us? Latterly, I have rather stopped worrying so much about this as Brian is probably dead by now. But no wonder I have spent so long in therapy. There's a lot of family history to unpick.

Hattie was an Essex girl. No, not from Barking. I can't tell you how many times I've heard that gag. She came from Maldon. A posh village near the sea, though her home was a bit of a menagerie. Animals everywhere you looked. There were even horses in the garden. You had to compete for attention in that environment. But Mum was a very striking apricot-coloured poodle. I know most dogs are a bit soppy about their mothers, but she was drop-dead glam.

So that makes me a cockapoo. First generation, Hattie would tell us proudly. She was a bit of a snob and a dog's pedigree mattered to her. Nowadays, of course, almost every other dog you meet in London is a cockapoo or a something-doodle. You can't move for them. But back in 2011, I was a genuine rarity. I was the first of my type to be seen on the common. People would come up to my humans and say, 'He's an unusual colour. What breed is he?' Even other dogs were curious to know what I was. Usually, they pretend not to give a shit about anything.

I find it hard to write about Hattie. We only had just over eight weeks together but they were a very intense two months. It was like we both knew that our time together was short and we did our best to cram an entire lifetime into the days we had. She wasn't the most demonstrative of mothers. She seldom went in for public displays of affection and I can only remember her once saying she loved me. But she went out of her way to teach me everything she thought I might possibly need. She even taught me how to read. I loved the Spot books. Happy days.

And what about me? I guess I'm an equal blend of my mum and dad. I've got my mum's colouring

– along with a big black blob on my left side – and my dad's ears. If you're being picky, you could say my paws are a bit big for my feet but I've got a friendly, curious face. People always say I look cute, which annoys me. What gets missed is that I'm actually fairly bright. Certainly a lot sharper than many politicians I've met. Most of them are total narcissists. Unaware of their own limitations and the damage they are doing. We'll come on to Liz Truss later.

I was always a bit of a dreamer. Even now I drive my humans mad by dawdling over a nice smell while they yell at me to rejoin them on a walk. But I can't help it. Actually, I can. If I wanted to rush back to where they were then I would. The thing is, I quite like taking life at my own pace. There's so much that I can't control that it's good to do so when I can. A reminder that I am my own dog.

That's why I've never quite understood border collies. They seem to make a virtue of obeying orders within half a second of them being issued. Have they not ever longed to ignore the whistles? To let the sheep do whatever they like. Let them go for a wander in the fields. Just for the hell of it. A bit of creative anarchy. Obviously, border collies get off on being told how clever they are. Every one I've ever met has gone on and on in a rather needy sort of way about how intelligent they are. Yet this is just another version of the patriarchy at work with the dogs near the bottom of the pecking order. Supposed to be grateful to be allowed on to the quad bike with the farmer. So, maybe border collies aren't as bright as they are cracked up to be. Just easily trained and bought off.

Most of my first few days were spent either asleep or feeding. But on about day five, my mother began to crack the whip. We weren't going to have a lot of time together as a family, she said, and there was a lot we needed to learn before we all went our separate ways. So the mornings were taken up with maths and basic English – she made sure we all learned to read: something for which I've always been grateful. I can't tell you the number of dogs I've met in later life who struggle with basic literacy skills. Imagine not being able to read a good thriller. Like *The Hound of the Baskervilles*. The afternoons were spent playing together and learning socialisation skills with the humans who looked after Mum.

It may surprise you, given my subsequent career in politics, but I was one of the shyest in the family. I wasn't at all pushy and was frequently bullied by my siblings. Ian and Jeff, in particular. They always seemed to take pleasure in me being the last to get fed. I guess you don't get to choose your siblings. I often wonder what became of them both. I hope they learned to chill out and didn't turn out like those gobby dogs you meet out on the common. Always thinking they are running the show and trying to order everyone else about. Stanley, Sophie and Lizzie were all sweethearts. They always had my back. And I like to think I had theirs.

And then, almost as soon as it had started, it was over. Our time together was up. 'Listen, everyone,' Mum said one day. 'I want you to know that I love you all very much. I may not always show it, but that's because I'm a dog. We're taught to be slightly detached from our puppies. Don't get me wrong, I'd fight anyone, do anything to keep you all alive. To give you whatever you need. But part of me has to keep my distance. Otherwise, it would be totally unbearable saying goodbye to you all.

'You see, we've reached that moment in our relationship when it's time to say goodbye. I've given you all everything I have. You're all very bright. Better educated than most humans. Best of all, you are all very decent dogs. You understand the difference between right and wrong. Even now, you know when you have done something bad. I couldn't be more proud of you. But now I have to let you go. To make your own way in the world. Just know that whatever you do, wherever you go, I will always be with you. Cheering you on.'

Hattie fell silent and wiped a paw across her eyes. The fur at the back my neck tingled. This was it. Life was about to get serious. I didn't feel at all ready for this. Mum went on to spell out just how our departures would be choreographed. It was like this. All six of us puppies would be put in a cardboard box. Then some humans who were looking to be adopted would enter the room and be allowed to play with us. After however long it took, they would make their decision.

And then one of us would be gone. It sounded terrifying.

The first to go was Ian. Of course it was. Always pushing himself to the front. No sooner had he caught sight of the humans than he was barging the rest of us out the way. Bouncing up and down and leaping up against the box. Shouting, 'Me, me, me,' as loud as he could. Mind you, he didn't look quite so pleased with himself when he dropped by to collect his stuff and say goodbye to us all. His lips were quivering, and he could barely whisper. On his way out, he gave us a pathetic little wave. That was the last I ever saw of him.

Sophie was the next to go. Then Jeff. Then Stanley. There was just me and Lizzie left. One afternoon, while I was having a long snooze, Mum woke me up to have a word. 'I've been watching you, Eric . . .'

'Yes . . .' I didn't like the sound of where this conversation was going.

'Look me in the eyes, Eric. Don't piss about. This is serious. Why is it that whenever humans turn up to choose a puppy, you're always lurking at the back of the box? Doing everything possible not to draw attention to yourself? How do you think you are going to find a human to own?'

I stammered out a reply. 'I j-j-just don't want to leave you,' I said. 'I like it here. I feel safe. I don't want a new family.'

'I thought so. But this is the way it's got to be. Don't make it even harder than it needs to be. Otherwise, you might end up with someone you don't like. Promise me this. That if the next humans look vaguely friendly – remember they will be as nervous as you – that you make an effort to give them a home. Promise?'

'Promise.'

So, the following Saturday, three humans pitched up to Maldon in a rackety old BMW estate. Two older ones, called Jill and John, and their teenaged son, Robbie. They looked nice enough, so I gave it my everything. Channelled my inner Ian. I did everything I could think of to get their attention. I dashed around the box like a blue-arsed fly and rolled on my back, yelling, 'Tickle my tummy.'

It worked a treat. They fell in love with me immediately. At least John did. Jill seemed to be having second thoughts. 'Look at the other one. She's really shy. I feel sorry for her. What if no one wants her?'

At this point, I lost it. 'For fuck's sake,' I shouted. 'Excuse my language. But really! Here am I going out of my way to act like an idiot to attract your attention and you're just worrying about Lizzie. She'll be absolutely fine.'

Jill wavered and gave in. She too wanted the bouncy one. She wanted me.

'Hello, Herbie,' she said.

'It's Eric,' I replied.

'Herbie.'

'Eric.'

'Herbie.'

'OK. Herbie it is.'

There was just time to say goodbye to Hattie for the last time. Though the words remained half formed in my mouth. What is there to say to a mother who has given you so much and you will never see again. I wanted time to stop. For me and Mum to be held in an everlasting kiss. But then I could hear John in the distance saying it was time to go. I tried to be the grown-up. Tried to fool myself that it was only for one night. That I would be back again tomorrow.

I tried to leave that room without a backward glance. But I couldn't do it. I swivelled my head for one last look at my mother. To capture a lifetime of maternal desire in a single moment. So I would never feel empty. Never feel lost. Never feel an unbearable need. Hattie stared back at me. Her lips locked in a silent, 'I love you.' Her eyes never left me until the door was finally closed.

Chapter 3

The journey to my new home can only have taken about two and a half hours, but it felt far longer. I was terrified, cooped up inside a cardboard prison, unable to look out the window and see where we were going. From time to time, Robbie, who was sitting on the back seat, would place his arm inside the box to stroke me gently and say, 'It's all right, Herbie. You're going to love Tooting.'

'I'll be the judge of that,' I said. Well, really. I didn't want to be churlish but how would you feel if you'd effectively been kidnapped and bundled into the back of a car. I mean, it's not the best of starts to a new relationship, is it?

Still, I must have dozed off for some of the ride – I'm a very good sleeper. It's one of my defence mechanisms. To blank out the world and hope everything is going to be OK when I wake up – because the time passed quickly enough and soon the car had pulled up

outside a semi-detached house in south-west London. They carried me in through the front door and took me into the living room. 'Welcome to your new home,' they all said. They meant well, but they sounded as anxious as I felt.

I don't mean to be churlish, but part of me was rather disappointed with where I had ended up. I had been hoping for so much more. A palace maybe. Or a four-storey town house with a big back garden. I never really wanted to live in the country. It's fine for visiting from time to time but it's too cold and wet. Not sure I'm quite tough enough for that. Too much of a metrosexual.

It's not just me. Most dogs I've met have grandiose tendencies. When you know that you're going to be bundled off to a strange place as a puppy, you can't help dreaming of where you might end up. It's only natural. I was talking about this when I went to visit my friends in Balmoral a while ago. They were telling me that corgis are particularly prone to delusional thinking, because they are taught at birth to believe they have won a ticket to the lottery of life. To be a corgi is to be in with a chance of being admitted to the royal family.

Obviously, the rest of us dogs never get a look-in, so it's not really an issue for us. But some corgis who have managed to convince themselves they are destined for greatness – dinner served by flunkeys every night – only to find they are outsourced to a one-bedroomed flat in St Alban's never really recover.

Some suffer from post-traumatic stress disorder. Some fly into terrible rages if other dogs don't automatically defer to them and let them go first through doors. I've yet to meet a corgi who hasn't needed therapy. Other than the late queen's.

Back to Tooting. Maybe it was just the greyness of a November afternoon. The sort where both the land and the sky merge into a dull monochrome. But I couldn't help feeling the house was one of the ugliest I had ever seen. A chipped and fading mock-Tudor facade. Whoever thought that was a good idea? John and Jill had clearly lived here a while so why hadn't they bothered to make it look nice? Why not replace the hideous lattice windows at the front? Or, at the very least, repair the wooden sills?

The inside was a little more promising. The rooms were large – here you could, at a push, make a case for the décor being homely and welcoming rather than borderline tatty. There's nothing worse than houses where the owners are so precious that you can't move without being shouted at for leaving paw prints on the carpet. Just chill out a little. You've got a Hoover. So, use it. Best of all, the rooms had plenty of bookshelves. I glanced at the titles. A wide selection of non-fiction along with plenty of nineteenth- and twentieth-century classics. I wasn't going to get bored. It appeared that we had similar tastes in literature.

I was just beginning to settle in a bit when two cats appeared through a hole in the wall. What the fuck? How come no one had warned me about this? Now,

I've nothing against cats in principle. No animus. The age-old hostility between cats and dogs has been rather overdone. We've all learned to grow up a bit. But even so, it would have been nice if someone had bothered to tell me I would be sharing a house with a couple of moggies. Just so I could have come prepared.

Still, John and Jill also hadn't taken the courtesy of telling the cats about me. They were horrified to see me. Jess, a tortoiseshell mix of some kind who clearly felt she was the boss cat, came over and spat in my face. Charming. Buzz, a neurotic black cat, just ignored me. Trying to make me disappear with a prolonged display of indifference. Sadly, I regret to say that our relationship never improved in the eleven years or so we shared the house. They both went on hating me every bit as much as they hated each other. You'd never have guessed they were sisters.

I blame them for the impasse. Trust me. As you get to know me better, you will discover I'm basically a very fair dog. When things are my fault, I usually own up. I can't help it. I've got an honest face. I never get away with anything. Though you can't say the same for all dogs. What was it that idiot Wittgenstein once said? It was in the philosophy 101 course that all dogs take as puppies. The difference between the consciousness of humans and of dogs is that dogs are incapable of dissimulating. We can't tell lies. Apparently.

Was Wittgenstein on drugs? Or was he just a half-wit? My mum told me it was just yet more evidence that humans don't understand dogs nearly as well as they think they do. Now, I will have to confess that I'm not the best liar myself, though I have got away with a surprising amount over the years. Humans tend to believe what they want to believe. But my friend Joey is in a league of his own. Utterly charming, but a complete delinquent. Other dogs suss him out immediately. Would never dream of leaving their phones or wallets out unattended. But humans only see an adorable cavalier King Charles spaniel. Even his own humans are fooled. He just puts on his innocent face and gets away with murder. The amount he has shoplifted.

Schopenhauer was another so-called intellectual who understood the human condition but was clueless when it came to dogs. Don't get me wrong. He was a decent enough bloke. You can't fault a man who adored poodles above all others. But his devotion left him blind to our real selves. He came to believe that dogs could only exist in the now. An ever-unfolding present. That we had no comprehension of the past or present. He thought we were all zen masters. If only. We might have a healthier attitude towards death but some of us still worry a lot. Nor do we forget. It takes a lot of hard work to be a dog. We take our mental health seriously. To just assume it all comes naturally to us is a huge error. A typically human response. The belief that humans are inherently superior. What a missed opportunity to learn from us.

Anyway, I digress. Back to Jess and Buzz . . . I never did really understand what was wrong with them.

You'd have thought they could at least be civil. I was only tiny when I arrived and was desperate to fit in. But they bullied me from the off. Sat on the stairs, looking aggressive, knowing I was too timid to tiptoe my way past.

Their behaviour never changed. It was almost as if they couldn't forgive me for being me. It was hyper-personal. It was my very existence to which they took exception. The only thing I could have done to improve our relationship was to not have been born. Even dying wouldn't have been good enough for them, as then they might occasionally be cursed with a memory of me.

The closest we ever came to a conversation was when Jess once said, 'I suppose you think you're special. That Jill and John love you more than they love us because you get to take them out for walks. Well, we hate you. We despise you. You're a complete loser.' It was weird. Often, I felt more alone in the house when they were guarding the living-room sofa than when there was nobody but me at home.

The sisters died within three months of each other at the age of eighteen. Or rather, they both went to Dignitas. Cancer. It was all a bit odd. Buzz was the first to take the one-way trip to the vet. She didn't moan. She almost seemed ready to go. But Jess looked totally unconcerned. When Buzz didn't come back, she showed no sign of missing her at all. If anything, she seemed almost pleased to have outlived her. In a funny kind of way, I think I was sadder when Buzz died than her sister was. And even I felt a bit guilty about how little I cared. When Jess died a few months later, it was almost a relief. As if a dark cloud had been lifted from the house.

For the first few hours in my new home I did my best to settle in. To try and get my bearings around the house. The stairs were tough, but my legs were just about long enough and I could manage them if I concentrated hard. The most annoying thing was the humans following me round, continually asking if I was OK and trying to stroke me. I appreciated their concern but, really, I wanted to be left alone for a bit. Just back off. Their neediness was becoming oppressive. Especially when I had my own issues to deal with. Eventually it got dark and we settled down to watch the TV together.

'What would you like to see?' asked John. 'Do you fancy a documentary on the Vietnam war? Or *101 Dalmatians*?'

'Mmm,' I replied. 'Give me the remote and let me see what else is on.'

He passed it over and I started scrolling. 'Perfect,' I said. 'There's a new series of *Silent Witness*. My absolute favourite. It was cult viewing at home in Essex. It's the only crime drama that gets less exciting the longer it goes on. By the end, you're barely awake. Which is just what I need on my first night in a new house.'

Then bedtime. John and Jill tucked me up in a furry basket, wished me goodnight and went upstairs. Now

I wasn't feeling so brave. Life was becoming just a bit too scary. Too real. I was on my own. It was me against the world. I tried to act like a grown-up and started unpacking. My hand came across something unexpected. It was a letter. I pulled it out and started reading.

My darling Eric,

By now you will be in your new home and I expect you will be feeling very anxious. You always were a worrier. But let me assure you that all will be well. I wouldn't have allowed John and Jill to take you away if I had thought they weren't going to take care of you. They are good people. Try to remember, this is also a new relationship for them. They too are finding their way and may make mistakes. But don't take this personally. It is also up to you to let them know what you need. You have a good heart, Eric. I could feel your kindness from the moment you were born. You have the potential to do great things. To be a dog who changes the world. You deserve all the good things that will come to you. Go and enjoy your life. Love and be loved. Know that I adored you from the moment I set eyes on you and I will do so as long as I live. Life won't always be easy. It never is. But whatever you do, be true to yourself. My love goes with you as your love stays with me. I will be cheering you on every step of the way.

With all my love, Mum

It was a bitter-sweet moment. I felt broken yet stronger. This was going to be OK. I started howling. Loud enough for my humans to hear. Not long afterwards they both came downstairs.

'What's up, Herbie?' asked Jill.

'I want to sleep upstairs with you, if that's OK. I get lonely on my own.'

'Of course you can join us. Just so long as you don't mind the noise. John does snore rather loudly. And I like the radio on in the morning.'

'That's fine. I won't take up too much room on the end of the duvet. Just don't get your feet in my face.'

And that's where I've been ever since. More or less. I like to roam a bit in the night, as I get twitchy. I start off on the bed for a goodnight snuggle. Then I bunker down at the top of the stairs, as I sometimes get a little warm. Occasionally, I might go into the spare room to stretch out on my own and to read. Jill gets very tetchy if anyone switches the light on. Then back to my main bed to wake everyone up. There's nothing they like more than my face on their pillow first thing.

'Really?' said Jill.

It wasn't long before we were a proper family unit. Certainly, a great deal more functional than many others I came to observe. Sure, we all occasionally rubbed each other up the wrong way, but nothing we couldn't resolve with a good chat. Mostly, I just felt the mutual love and the respect. And, not to put too fine a point on it, I think I can truthfully say that was largely down to me.

The trick was to treat Jill and John like idiots without allowing them to feel as if they were being treated that way. I don't mean to suggest they were stupid. More that they were inexperienced. They might both have had good jobs and been decent enough parents, but they had no idea how to look after me. All the knowledge they had was either mined from a book, *How To Look After Your Dog*, which wasn't worth the paper it was printed on, or had been passed on from their neurotic friends who had dogs with personality disorders.

So, it was left to me to gently explain what I expected of them. When I wanted my food. What I liked eating. How it should be served. When I wanted to be let out for a piss. Let's face it, would you like to go outside in the rain straight after dinner? And it worked out just fine. The humans could sense I was settling in and could congratulate themselves on what a brilliant job they were doing to train me. For some reason, they need to think they are the ones in control. Otherwise, they get very bad-tempered. Their powerlessness is an affront to their narcissism.

There was one last surprise in the early days. I discovered my humans were actually a pack of four when the front door opened and this young woman walked in.

'You must be Herbie,' she said.

'That's right,' I said. 'Who are you?'

'I'm Anna. I used to live here for eighteen years. I'm Jill and John's eldest child. I left home to go to university and no sooner was I out the door than you show up.'

'Them's the breaks . . . What do you expect me to do about it?'

'Er . . . Well, so long as you remember I'm more important than you . . .'

'I don't think so. Things have moved on round here.'

'But . . . But I'm their daughter . . .'

'Look. Relax a bit. Try to think of it as a life lesson. The dynamics change in any family. They don't love you any less. They just love me a little more. Part of my role is to help them to miss you less. Why don't we just have a hug and stop fighting. Share the love, Anna. Deal?'

'Deal.'

I rolled on to my back and let her scratch my tummy. Never fails.

Some weeks later, the routine was in place. Jill and John were just about ready to be allowed to be taken for a walk. I clipped the lead to my collar and placed the other end in Jill's hand. This was heaven. The sights. The smells. The dogs. The people. The grass on Tooting Bec Common was somehow the greeniest green I had ever seen. And the sticks were the woodiest wood. I was amazed that humans could just ignore them. How come they didn't throw them to one another and run to pick them up? Then there was the pondiest pond and the muddiest mud. Life could never be better than this, I thought. Very heaven to be alive in the moment.

Looking back, I can see I rather let myself down in the first few months of these walks. But I was young. Still a very impressionable puppy. I would run up to every dog I met and pester them to play with me. It didn't occur to me that for many dogs, the walk was a part of their daily meditation. A time to be alone with nature. To think things through. They don't want to be bothered by some hyperactive puppy with ADHD. But, in time, I calmed down. We all do. Though some of us need meds. It's a state of mind. I know when I go out in the morning that I'm almost certainly going back to Tooting Bec Common. But I still feel the same sense of excitement as I did in the early days. I never get bored of it. There's always something new. A squirrel that wasn't there the day before. The smell of the rain on the leaves. The pleasure to be found in small things. Humans could learn from this.

And so, the days merged into weeks into months into years. Life settled into a comfortable routine. I like routines. They soothe my anxiety. Best of all, I felt loved. Safe. Sometimes a whole day would go past without me even thinking of my mum.

Chapter 4

Try to see things my way. Now, a day for you is no big deal. Some may drag, others may race past but, on the whole, it's not a huge chunk out of your life. But for us dogs it's a bit different. As I said a while back, one human day is like roughly a week to us. This isn't a moan. It's not special pleading. Just an observation. To let you know that things can get boring.

So, much as I enjoyed my life with Jill and John, there were times when I was overcome with ennui. There were days when Jill was off running a division of a literacy charity and John was working in Westminster when I had nothing to do but snooze and sit on my bum. OK, so that might be a bit of an exaggeration. I also got to watch TV and scroll through Twitter on the phone John had bought me. You can waste hours looking at videos of humans doing dumb things.

I also did a lot of reading. Fiction mainly but also quite a lot political and social history of the twentieth and twenty-first centuries. A dog has to keep his mind active. One of the first books John lent me was *Flush* by Virginia Woolf, a supposed biography of Elizabeth Barrett Browning's cocker spaniel. Between you and me, I actually found it a bit annoying. You can have too much overwrought stream of consciousness. Everyone needs a bit of downtime when not every feeling is critically important. No wonder Flush went on to bite Robert Browning. He was desperate to escape his rarified gilded cage and his opium-addicted human.

From there, I moved on to Dickens. A great bloke who was obsessed with dogs. Though I will never forgive him for his portrayal of Jip in *David Copperfield*. A lapdog almost as idiotic as her owner, Dora. I'm sure I wasn't the only one who let out an almighty cheer when she was killed off. There were plenty of other dogs in Dickens to keep me amused. As there were elsewhere in Victorian literature. So, I became something of an expert on nineteenth-century English fiction. Shame it's now out of favour in so many university English departments. Otherwise I might have had a career in academia.

I wouldn't want you to think I was neglected. I wasn't. I had plenty to do in the day, meeting up with friends and taking them for walks and, on their days off and in the evenings, I would sometimes take John and Jill on the bus into town to go to a gallery – all three of us were very keen on British studio ceramics – or to the opera. I once starred in a production of *La Fille du Regiment* at the Royal Opera House. Not the greatest music ever written but I was sensational. My walk across the stage into the soprano's arms completely stole the show. Everyone said I should have won an award for it.

But the truth is, I was at a loose end. I know, I know. I can hear the objections. He doesn't know how lucky he was. Spoiled brat. And it's true, I was living on easy street. I had a loving family and a nice house. I didn't go hungry. I was allowed to do pretty much what I wanted. I even had my own laptop. But it wasn't enough. I wasn't one of those dogs who enjoyed doing as little as possible all day. And I certainly didn't want to be a show dog, sitting for hours every day under a fur dryer while my hair was coiffed and primped. At the back of my mind, I could hear my mother's voice getting ever louder. Follow your dreams. Be the best version of yourself.

There was only one thing for it. It was time to get a job. But what? We may be living in more enlightened times now, but there is still a lot of prejudice against dogs. Humans are still far too ready to just pigeon-hole us as animals. As if we had the consciousness of a squirrel. If we're lucky, we get classified as pets. Such a condescending term. Humans have no idea how patronising they can be. Still blissfully unaware that it's we who are doing them the favour. Sometimes we're the only thing holding a family together. How unobservant must you be to think we are much the same as a cat or a guinea pig. In some so-called civilised countries, humans even like to eat dogs. We're a culinary speciality. How barbaric is that? I can't even begin to comprehend that mentality. That someone could look at me and think lunch. You won't catch me visiting those countries.

Like many dogs I know, I initially dreamed of being an athlete. I was nearly one when the Olympics came to London in 2012 – younger dogs are amazed that I was alive for this – and John and I watched nearly every minute on TV. It was an inspiration to me. During the day, we would go out to the common and use our walk as interval training. Sprint repetitions followed by thirty seconds recovery. You should try it. Totally knackering. But even though I ended up one of the fastest medium-sized dogs in the borough, that still wasn't good enough.

John took me down to the dog track in Wimbledon to join the running club, but it wasn't really for me. Just greyhound after greyhound. Whip-thin and VO_2 levels to die for from decades of inbreeding. There was no chance of me ever competing at that level. The chief coach – a former champion greyhound called Stan – was very nice and encouraging. 'It's not about the winning,' he would say. 'It's about improving your personal best.' But I did rather feel as if he was humouring me. There was no fun to be had from coming in fifty metres behind all the other dogs in every race.

It got to the point where I started inventing injuries. 'My knee hurts,' I would say, halfway through the warm-ups. Trying to remember which side to limp on. After about nine months, John got the hint and stopped making me go every Tuesday and Thursday evening. A shame really, as I think I did have talent. Just not racing greyhounds. It always amazed me that humans didn't get round to organising competitions for other breeds. They go to enormous lengths to devise different categories for themselves. So, it wouldn't have hurt to create an eight-hundred-metre steeplechase for cockapoos.

This was the dark ages for dogs, though. Some would argue that we are still in them. Most humans can only imagine dogs in strict stereotypes. Conforming to a prescribed view of the world. Now this suits some mutts down to the ground. I've mentioned sheepdogs before. They love nothing more than rounding up sheep in the pouring rain while some lazy human stands several hundred yards away and blows a whistle. Well, that's not me. I am not that dog. I want more from my life than that. Some collies can't even read.

Nor do any of the other typical job openings for dogs appeal. I don't want to join the police. I quite like the idea of catching criminals, but the bureaucracy would get to me – all that form filling – and I'm not sure I would survive in the current culture of the Metropolitan police. I'm too woke. I couldn't stand the casual racism. You can't ignore that kind of stuff when you are mixed-race yourself. Nor would I like to be a gun dog. Jumping into rivers to fetch a dying pheasant after a human has shot it out of the sky. Nah. If you want to kill birds then you can go and find their bodies yourself.

I did briefly think about signing up to become a guide dog. It must be nice to be that useful. To be someone else's eyes. I even went on an open day to see if I might like it. But in the end, I didn't think I had the patience. I like being my own dog too much. I'll be the judge of what I think is a good idea. It wouldn't be long before my blind human and I would fall out. 'Time to go outies,' he would say. 'Give it fifteen minutes,' I would reply. 'It's tipping down at the moment.' I rather suspect that kind of attitude would be a fail.

Apart from anything else, I didn't want a job where I would have to move house and switch human. I'd got used to the chipped paint of Chateau Tooting and I had become very fond of Jill and John. They had proved very obliging at adapting to my routine. No, what I wanted was the sort of job that most humans had. One where you left the house in the morning and came back again at night. Was that really so much to ask for?

There was nothing for it but hard slog. Endless online application forms. Usually demanding qualifications that I didn't have. I may be well read and a lot brighter than most humans but I haven't got a university degree to show for it. Bizarrely, no one was very interested in my thoughts on nationalism in nineteenth-century opera. Nor that I was numerate and up to speed with current affairs. I always watched the 10 o'clock news on the TV, read most of the papers online and even tuned into the BBC Parliament channel for prime minister's questions and important ministerial statements and urgent questions. You could call me a politics nerd. Out on walks, I would frequently get into arguments with the more right-wing dogs from the posh side of the common. Explain to me, I would say, how the Conservatives can blame Labour for the financial crash when at the time they were the ones who had been shouting for greater deregulation. They never really had an answer. Just called me a lefty and said you could never trust Labour with the economy. I bet their parents and their parents' parents had said that too.

I did get a few jobs. A part-time gig at the local coffee shop, trying to be charming to the hipsters and the yummy mummies who had moved into the area for the schools. Charity fundraising. Standing around in the street hoping to catch the attention of people doing their utmost to avoid you. Then the pretend conversation before getting them to sign up to a monthly commitment that most will cancel the moment they get home. Jobs don't get much more dispiriting than that. Night-time shelf stacking at the supermarket. You name it, I've given it a go. You can't call me lazy or work-shy.

John and Jill were very good about it. Telling me not to worry so much. That there still was a lot of anti-dog prejudice and it was OK for me not to do very much. They were happy to subsidise my lifestyle. I actually didn't cost them that much. Just my food, my haircuts every three months and the odd day out with Mike, the dog walker. In fact, they quite liked having me around the house. They found it somewhat reassuring to find me asleep at the top of the stairs. Or doing Wordle on my laptop.

But it wasn't OK for me. I felt as if something was missing from my life. I felt unfulfilled. Sure, it was great to love and to be loved but that wasn't quite enough. I wanted a job that mattered to me. One that could make a difference. It didn't have to be tremendously well paid. I wasn't interested in working for Goldman Sachs. I just wanted to be able to look myself in the eye. To have a job that, in however small a way, left the world a slightly better place than I found it.

Then, just as I was on the verge of giving up – of resigning myself to being yet another Essex-Boy-made-good, a member of the kept middle-classes, I caught a break. I was out with Jill having a nice dawdle, taking even longer over the smells than usual, when I bumped into a friend. Lunar, the black labrador who owned Sadiq Khan, our local member of parliament. We said hi to one another and started to chat.

'What's up?' I asked. 'Seen any new dogs out and about?'

This was generally the first question all dogs in Tooting asked. There're always at least two or three new ones a month.

'Not today,' said Lunar. 'But there might be big changes ahead at home. Between you and me, if Labour don't win the next election in 2015 – and frankly who is betting on that? – then Sadiq is thinking of running for London Mayor.'

'That's amazing. So, you will get to be the Mayoral Dog? Maybe your own basket in County Hall?'

'One step at a time, Herbs. But what about you?'

'Not so great. To tell you the truth, I'm a bit depressed. I just can't find a decent job.'

'Really. Well as it happens, I might be able to help. You know Ed Miliband?'

'Sure . . .'

'He's looking for someone to help him out. He's really struggling with his public image. Half the country thinks he's Red Ed and the other half thinks he's a clown. So not great. Anyway, he wants a new person to join his leader of the opposition team in Westminster. Someone he can trust for advice and who will help out with his speech writing. Someone different from the usual Oxbridge gene pool. Someone capable of thinking out of the box. What do you think?"

'Sounds ideal. So, what should I do?'

'Drop him an email. Tell him I suggested you get in touch. See what happens. I think you'll be great.'

'You're a star, Lunar. Thank you so much. And good luck with becoming London Mayor.'

On my return home I started composing the email. But soon got stuck. Somehow, I just couldn't persuade myself that I was the best dog for the job. It was that old glass ceiling that all mutts come up against. I didn't know if I could do it because I had never met another dog doing something similar. I felt trapped. Angry with myself. I closed the laptop and went to have a snooze in front of the TV. Maybe I would feel better when I woke up.

I didn't. I felt worse. I couldn't even eat my dinner. My head was all over the place. Caught between ambition and reality. But was this really it? If I didn't take this chance, I might never get another. It was Jill and John who came to the rescue. Beckoning me to join them on the sofa.

'What's the matter, Herbie?' said Jill. 'You just don't seem yourself.'

So I told them.

Jill talked me through it. 'I've felt the same way,' she said. 'There have been times when I wasn't sure whether I could do a job. But the thing is you will never know unless you try. Maybe you will get an interview but still they turn you down. Then no harm done. Just a little bit of wounded pride. And if you do get the job and later decide it's not for you, then you can always quit. My advice is to go for it.'

'But you do realise that if I get the job then there will have to be changes to our lifestyle,' I said. 'The hours will be brutal. I'll have to get you up to take you for a walk much earlier. And it's possible you might get the media hanging around the house from time to time . . .'

'That's fine,' said John. 'We'll cope. We just want you to lead your best life. We made a promise to your mum and we meant it. We always felt that you were special.'

So, I quickly dashed off the email – confident but not cocky – and crossed my paws. I was a nightmare to live with for the next few days, constantly checking my emails on the phone. I tried to give the impression that I wasn't that bothered. That however it turned out was fine by me. That just sending off the application was an achievement in itself. But inside I was a mess. Now that I had sent the email, I really wanted the job.

Two days later a reply came back from Ed. 'Sounds interesting. Why not come in to my office in Norman Shaw North to discuss? Does 11 tomorrow morning suit?'

I went mad. Running round and round the kitchen, barking loudly. My barks didn't even make sense to me. They were just expressions of pure joy.

'What do you think I should wear?' I asked.

'I should imagine your black and white fur will do just fine,' John said. 'You don't have the shiny blue suit that is the uniform of every other special adviser in Westminster. But if I was you, I would have a shower first. You've got mud all over your legs.'

That evening, we watched a couple of early episodes of *The West Wing* to get me in the mood, but I could hardly sleep. Instead, I paced anxiously round the house trying to anticipate every question. Inevitably, I arrived at Portcullis House far too early – it was the one day of the month when there were no delays on the Northern line – and presented myself to the security guards.

'Who are you?' they asked, aggressively.

'Herbert Hound.'

'Course you are. Who are you coming to see?'

'Ed Miliband.'

They didn't seem to believe me. Why is there still this rampant dogophobia in society? I get so tired of fighting it. Day in, day out. People constantly trying to put us down. In the background I could hear the security officer calling Ed's office. 'We've got a Mr Hound in reception. Says he's got an appointment with you. Oh, he has. That's fine. Sorry to have bothered you. You'll send someone down to collect him?'

'OK, Mr Hound. Just put your mobile through the scanner and wait over there.'

I was kept waiting for about twenty minutes before a rather lean and sweaty man finally appeared.

'Follow me, Dog,' he said brusquely, not looking me in the eyes.

Charming. This must be Dan. Ed's right-hand man. His reputation preceded him. A man with evident anger-management problems. Who regarded the *Thick of It* as an instruction manual. But nothing I couldn't handle. In my time, I've taken on several furious XL bullies. Though now wasn't the time to take him on. No point in making enemies on day one. I could neutralise him later.

I followed Dan up the stairs to Ed's second-floor office, passing lots of people all trying to look busier and more important than the next person. I even caught sight of Iain Duncan Smith in the corridor. Imagine the state of the Conservative Party to have once elected him as their leader.

Ed rushed to greet me. A mix of hair and teeth. Rather better-looking in real life than he often appeared on the television.

'Thank you for coming in, Herbert . . .'

'Herbie. You can call me Herbie . . .'

'Herbie. Can I get you a drink, Herbie? A cappuccino? A flat white . . .?'

'A bowl of water will do just fine. And some biscuits if you've got any?'

'Sure. Still or sparking?

'Sparkling, please.'

I could get to like this. I was feeling good. I liked Ed. He had a way of making you feel good about yourself. We had a bit of small talk about the family and then got to the nitty-gritty.

'So, what makes you think that you are right for my team?' he said. 'That you can manage my comms team. There's under a year to go till the next election and I've still got an image problem with some voters. There's not much time to make a difference.'

I paused. I had been expecting this question and I wanted to make sure he heard my answer. 'I'm going to be honest with you, Ed,' I said. 'I will never just tell you what I think you want to hear. It's like this. You've tried countless different people on your comms team and none of them have worked out. If you just pick another identikit young man or woman, then you are definitely going to lose the election. It's time to try something radical. I'm not going to bullshit you. You might still lose the election if you do hire me. But at least you will be in with a chance.'

I could see that what I had said had hit home. That Ed's own research and gut instinct were telling him the same thing. 'But why you . . .?'

'How many other dogs do you know who could do the job? I've got the ideas. I share your principles. I believe in social justice and a better society for everyone. Most of all, I've got the skills. People instinctively like me. I've got a face they can trust. What's more, I can extend your core base. If you don't mind me saying, you're very north London. You give the impression you've never crossed the river. But I was born in Essex and moved to south London when I was just eight weeks old. People relate to me. I bark their language.'

'Hmm . . .' Ed dithered.

'You know I'm right.'

'Just one thing . . . can you drive? It could be handy for getting from meeting to meeting.'

I stared at him quizzically. 'You do know I'm a dog, don't you? My feet can't reach the pedals.'

'Of course, of course. That isn't a deal breaker.' There was silence for about twenty seconds. It felt longer. 'OK,' he said eventually. 'Let's do it. I trust

Lunar and I trust you. You are someone whom I will enjoy working with. And as you said, what have I got to lose? Without big changes, the Tories will probably win next May anyway. So, let's do it. What do you say, Herbie?'

I could have hugged Ed. Instead, I just wagged my tail.

'Welcome to the team, Herbie. Dan, help him get his security pass sorted.'

One small step for a dog. One giant leap for dogkind.

Chapter 5

Work wasn't initially as much fun as I'd hoped.

It wasn't the routine I minded. In fact, I rather enjoyed that aspect. The excitement of waking up in the morning knowing I was headed off to Westminster never left me. The thrill of the walk to the Tube. Checking my emails and messages, trying to keep up with any breaking news. Heading to the special underground entrance to parliament that was only accessible to pass holders. The morning meeting at which we updated the daily grid. Outside visits: I've always enjoyed a train and car ride. The preparation for prime minister's questions. The afternoon nap on my office chair looking out the window at the boats on the Thames. I never tired of any of that.

What got to me was the people. Especially the special advisers and researchers who swarmed through the atrium of Portcullis House en route to their MP's office. All the men appeared to be called Tom, Ben or Richard. All the women, Lucy, Emma or Camilla. Many of them looked like they were fresh out of Oxbridge. Or a Russell Group university at a stretch. The rest had spent a few years at a think tank or a lobbying firm. Almost no one I met had had what you might call an ordinary job. Everyone was looking over everyone else's shoulder for someone more important to talk to. This was a place where a lot of talking got done but not much listening.

Even that I could have tolerated. I suppose it's only natural that a place like Westminster will attract those drawn to power. It was like a primal force running through the building. SpAds and researchers plotting their man or woman's progression up the ladder. Who was up? Who was down? In or out of the cabinet or shadow cabinet? Who was a backbencher for life? Which seats would be vacant at the next election? Who stood the best chance of getting on the candidates' list for a constituency? What you seldom heard were ideas for improving the country. Other than as a means for keeping power or grabbing it.

No. What bothered me most was that almost everyone – I'm not talking about Ed Miliband here or most of his shadow cabinet, more his entourage – seemed to look down on me. As if working with a dog was somehow beneath them. Now, I expected some prejudice when I joined Ed's team. All dogs get it now and again. Humans who don't want to share their space with us. Who think we are lesser beings. I've even had it from other dogs. I've had it from both sides. From pedigree dogs who think they are above mongrels – you get this especially round the time Crufts is on the TV – and from regular mutts who reckon that cockapoos are just a poncey middle-class hybrid. You can't win.

Weirdly, the attitude was most engrained in those who liked to pride themselves on their tolerance. It took Dan at least six months to call me by my name. Before that he just yelled 'Dog' at me. And seemed to think it was funny. The rest of the team were nice to me, but only in the way they might be kind to any dog. Offering me a biscuit and tickling me under the chin. Which, in its proper time and place, might have been welcome.

But this was my workplace. I don't want to get too Me Too about this and I'm not a dog who is overly bothered by my pronouns. You get used to people misgendering you and saying, 'Who's a good girlie then?' But the fact is that work is not the time for these displays of affection. I mean, I wouldn't go and sit on their laps and start nudging them for a cuddle when they were making a presentation. Nor would I lie back in my seat and start licking my cock during PMQs. There are codes of behaviour for a reason. And what someone is really doing when they start touching you at work without permission is demonstrating that they are your boss. That they are more powerful than you. That they can treat you as they wish.

All I really wanted was a sense of equality. To be treated with respect. For it to be understood that I might have the same hopes and dreams as they did. Not quite true this. Unlike almost everyone else with a green 'SpAd and researcher' pass, I didn't consider this job as a step on the ladder to becoming an MP. I couldn't think of much worse. Your prime purpose as a back-bencher is to support your party even when you think the leader is doing something idiotic and to get the odd mention in your local newspaper. And if you make it to the ranks of minister, it gets even worse as you have to be prepared to humiliate yourself by insisting that everything is fine when it so obviously isn't. I've lost count of the number of seemingly able Tory ministers whom I've heard crash and burn on the morning media round. It must be days before they dare show their faces in public again. I've never worked out if they have an excess of self-worth to do this or none at all.

But like everyone in Westminster, I wanted my voice to be heard. OK, I wanted others to acknowledge that I, too, can make a difference. That I have ideas and opinions that deserve to be heard. That I'm not just some dog who owes his job to someone else's diversity and equality agenda. In the early days, I tended to just suck it up. To take it on the chin. I didn't want people to think I was the new Big Dog on the block, throwing my weight around. I wanted to get the measure of the place. To show some humility. Let them see I was prepared to learn the rules and customs. To earn people's respect.

One day, though, I just lost it. We were all in the morning meeting and one of the Lucys, I'm not sure which as they both looked alike, was droning on about some new polling we had commissioned that showed Ed's support was flatlining with C1s in the Red Wall seats. The research was both really tedious and a statement of the bleeding obvious but somehow Lucy was trying to make out it held the key to the next election. And everyone else was just nodding along because they hadn't really been listening and wanted to make out that the findings tallied with their own data. Then right at the end, Lucy leant over, rubbed my head affectionately and said, 'And what do you think, Herbs?'

It was the way she said it that got to me. Playful. Patronising. Not like she was really interested. So, I told her. It was quite unlike me. Normally I'm rather a polite dog.

'You want to know what I really think? Well, let me tell you. Starting with this bullshit research that tells us nothing we didn't already know. Why are we even wasting time on this? We should be getting out and about and trying to change people's minds.

'But I'll tell you what I also think. That none of you really take me seriously because I'm a dog. You just assume you know better than me and that a dog couldn't possibly know more than you. Well, you may be right. I may not have any new insights. But the thing is, you would never really know. Try listening to me first before instantly dismissing me. Try to think your way past my cute face and the tail that never stops wagging.

'Think about it this way. If you're all so bloody clever, if you've all got all the answers, then how come Labour isn't way ahead in the polls. All the coalition of the Tories and the Lib Dems has to offer is austerity. Cutting public services that have already been cut to the bone. And you're just letting them get away with it. Their narrative that Labour caused the financial crash is winning. Whatever happened to the idea that Labour rescued the global economy? That the Tories had been in favour of even greater deregulation.

'Which brings us to Ed. The elephant in the room. Why is that no one really seems to know what he represents? How come we haven't moved on from the right-wing media's view of him as part of some out-of-touch north-London elite? The best that you lot have come up with was that 'One Nation' nonsense a few years back. It sounded good at the time but no one really knew what it meant. You said that Ed would come to spell out his vision of 'One Nation' over the coming months but he never did.

'So here we are. About a year out from the election and you're just treading water. So, don't take the piss out of me or patronise me for being a dog. Because if you're the finest political minds Labour can cobble together right now, then maybe a dog is what is needed.'

At some point during this outburst, my front paws had worked their way on to the glass table. Not the best look. I hastily removed them and sat back down on my chair. There was an awkward silence, with everyone staring at the floor. Somebody say something, please, I thought. Why had I done it? I asked myself. I had never meant to say all that. Had promised myself I would keep my thoughts to myself and just nod along. Be a Yes Dog. Now I'd almost certainly ended my career before it had even started. No one liked a gobshite.

Only it turned out they did. Who knew?

It was Ed who finally spoke. 'I think Herbie might have a point. Plenty for us all to think about here.'

'Absolutely,' chipped in Dan. 'Well said.'

'Yes, totes brill,' said Lucy and Ben.

I'd got away with it. I tried to look relaxed. As if the meeting had been no big deal. Though it's not easy for a dog to look dignified when he's climbing down out of a chair that is a little too high for him.

'Fancy joining us for lunch in the canteen?' said Dan.

A breakthrough. No one had ever invited me to socialise with them before. I didn't really fancy it. I much prefer to wolf down my food on my own while reading a book. But now wasn't the time to appear ungrateful. Spirit of comradeship. Reaching out and all that HR stuff. And the truth was I was pleased to be included.

It was weird, though. Suddenly I was a member of the in-crowd. People I wanted to like me were now taking me seriously. As if what I had said had been profound. When the reality was that I had only said what every other dog had been saying on Tooting Bec Common for months. Well, maybe not every dog. There was always Joey. He was never very political. He only ever took an interest on Budget day. And then only how a tax cut might lower the price of dog food. Not whether public services might be affected. But to the rest of us, it had been blindingly obvious that there was something badly wrong with the Labour Party machine. We talked about this frequently on our morning walks while our humans were in the cafe getting a coffee.

Still, maybe I wasn't so out of place as I had at first thought. Because in many ways most of Westminster are only dogs in human form. Pack animals, happily congregating themselves around an alpha male. Or sometimes an alpha female. It didn't matter whether the alpha was actually right or not. Only that they were perceived to be right. To be in the ascendancy. One of the Chosen Ones destined for great things. There was no great self-reflection on any of this. Everything was taken at face value. If people thought you were the alpha, you were the alpha. Until such a time that you weren't. Then you got dumped and everyone moved on to the newest, shiniest alpha. There was no shame in having attached yourself to someone who went on to lose their alpha status, because the pack mentality had to be maintained. The self-delusion. Every day was Day Zero in Westminster. A tabula rasa. Always looking forward, never back.

It's one of the political world's greatest achievements. And, also, its fault line. But for now, I had become one of the alphas. A junior alpha, but an alpha, nonetheless. A leader of the pack.

Talking of which, in the afternoon I got a tap on the back from Dan. Would I like to join him on his daily patrol round the offices of all the lobby journalists? He said it in a way that suggested no wasn't an answer. But besides this, I was quite curious to witness one first-hand. Others who had done this tour of duty had come back scarred for life. This was the stuff of legend.

We headed out at about 4 pm. First stop was *The Times* office. Dan wasted no time.

'What are you splashing with tomorrow?' . . . 'That's a fucking crap story. Why aren't you doing something on Labour's energy policy?'

It was the same as we wandered round the other newspaper offices. Dan would deliver a potty-mouthed rant on the state of British politics while the assembled hacks would either ignore him or respond with passive-aggressive grunts.

On the way back to the leader of the opposition's office, I timidly suggested to Dan that this might not be the best way to secure positive coverage. Maybe a bit more charm . . . a bit more interest in other people . . . and the papers might be more receptive. Dan wasn't having any of it. They were all bastards. All controlled by owners and editors who hated Labour. The only way to get through to them was to shout at them.

I decided to let it go. Maybe he had a point. Though I couldn't help feeling he had taken Malcolm Tucker as his role model a bit too seriously. And I've always regretted not saying something to Ed. Just in case he didn't know. Whatever Dan was doing, it wasn't working. Ed was getting consistently bad press. Though many of the papers were at their worst when the opinion polls were at their closest.

But if my work life was looking up now I was getting a bit more respect, things at home were a little more tricky. Though it took me a while to notice. You know how it is. You're working long hours, getting home late. You just want to eat your dinner and watch a bit of TV. You can't help taking your family for granted. You've got a vague sense that things are a bit off – your humans act a bit weird or needy around you – but you're tired so you decide to ignore it. Hope it will go away. That things will blow over by tomorrow. Only they don't. The niggles are still there.

It was Jill who brought things to a head. It was a Thursday night and I was lying on my back, stretched out on the living-room floor while watching *Question Time*. Jill was stroking my tummy but really I wanted to be left alone. I was trying to concentrate.

'We need to talk,' she said.

This sounded ominous. I put the TV on pause.

'You know that John and I love you very much,' she continued.

Er . . . Yes. Obviously. I am adorable.

'Yeah. And I love you both, too.'

'Well, it's just . . . How can I put it? When we got you . . .'

What? You got me? How many times do I have to tell you it was the other way round? I chose you.

'When we got you, we wanted a dog who was at home most of the time. A puppy to look after and keep us company . . .'

Puppy? How many times do I have to tell you I'm not a puppy. I'm nearly three years old.

'So, the thing is . . . we're feeling a bit neglected. Taken for granted even. You act as if you own the place . . .'

Category error. I'm fairly sure I do own the place.

'Do you think that when you are here, you could be a little more emotionally available?

I was fairly confident that most dogs don't have these conversations with their humans, but I felt that Jill had a point. Maybe I had been a bit selfish. And I did really love them. The last thing I wanted to do was upset them. Yes, they could have tidied up the place a bit for me but this was still home. We were a team. Me, Jill, John and the other two.

'I'm sorry,' I said. 'I should have consulted you more. But the job rather crept up on me and caught me by surprise. One moment I was just lying around not doing much apart from the odd walk and the next I find myself at the centre of Westminster political life. I hadn't planned any of this. It was just when the opportunity arose, I couldn't turn it down. It was where I was meant to be. I'm just not a stay-at-home kind of dog.'

'And we understand that,' Jill nodded, tickling my chin. 'We want you to be the best dog you can be. We're really proud of what you are doing. But just maybe you could text us when you're going to be late back. And be more present when you are here.'

'Of course,' I said. Licking her forehead. Doing my best soppy eyes. I give good soppy eyes. 'I didn't mean to hurt your feelings. Love you.'

'Love you, too. By the way, did you notice that John has gone mad?

'Again? What's he done this time?'

'He's only gone and got a tattoo of you on his arm.'

'You're kidding me.'

I raced over to where John was sitting and gave him a nudge. 'Come on,' I said. 'Show us.' John rolled up his left sleeve to reveal a huge tattoo of a dog.

'That's hideous,' I laughed. 'It looks nothing like me.'

'It's a cartoon version of you,' John said.

'It makes me look really fat. And dim. And what's that cigar doing in my paw?'

'It's not a cigar. It's a stick.'

'Oh . . . Well, if you're pleased with it, I suppose that's all that matters.'

'I thought you would be flattered.'

Actually, I was. There aren't many dogs who end up as a tatt on their human's arm. Even if it's a shit tatt. But John had another think coming if he thought I was going to reciprocate. There was no way I was getting one of him.

I was also getting some flak from the other dogs out on the common. They had misinterpreted my vaguely distracted air on walks and concluded that I was getting a bit up myself.

'Off to lose the next election?' snapped Ralph. A usually friendly, if completely fucked-up greyhound.

'Too important to chase sticks with us?' sighed Frida, one of my closest friends and the cleverest schnauzer I had ever met. She had two honorary degrees.

That hurt. As with Jill and John, I hadn't meant to upset the gang. It was just mission creep. What had begun with the excitement and intensity of a fulfilling new job was in danger of becoming a pathology. The last thing I wanted was to become as self-regarding as some of those I came across in Westminster. So, I apologised. I'd try not to be like that again, I told them. And please tell me if I am. Much better than letting the bad feeling fester. I am not good with bad feelings. Most dogs aren't.

But maybe things work out for a reason. Having my family and friends on my back shook me up. Reminded me that I wasn't some political Svengali pulling all the strings. That I wasn't a self-invented member of the Westminster in-crowd. And thank God for that. After all, no one likes a Dominic Cummings. Poor Dom. Convinced he's a genius, he now sits in his attic all day typing long screeds of nonsense that go unread. His sole purpose is to be laughed at. No, I was just one of a cast of thousands in the bubble. Though I was, it has to be said, the only dog.

The weeks drifted into months and I gradually settled into a routine. I like routines. I can get really naggy if I'm made to wait for a walk. Humans often forget who is doing whom the favour. Tuesdays were my favourites. You'd get individual members of the shadow cabinet coming in at various points in the week, but Tuesday was the day they were all there for the weekly meeting and I gradually got to know some of them quite well.

Ed Balls was actually a bit of a bore. Everything was always all about him and he liked everyone to know that he was the *grand fromage*. He was the shadow chancellor and you were no one. Imagine being that competitive with a dog. Harriet Harman was a sweetie but a bit too serious. No real sense of the absurd. Vernon Coaker aka Big Vern was a lot of fun as was Hilary Benn, with whom I'd commiserate over the latest Spurs disaster. But the loveliest of all was Rachel Reeves. This might surprise you as she has a reputation for being boring. I thought she was wonderful. She was by far the brightest person in any room but she never talked down to anyone and was always interested in what I had to say.

There was, though, an undeniable sense of drift during this period. A phoney war. We all knew we were heading for a general election in May of the following year and it was as if we were all marking time until then. Not so much a shadow cabinet, more shadow boxing. Everyone just trying not to make a mistake. Trying to stay fit till the big day. No one really daring to commit to any policy just in case it got shot down in flames and inadvertently started the campaign proper. The Tories were no different. They knew their coalition with the Lib Dems had reached the end of its shelf life and were now wondering how best to present themselves to the electorate. David Cameron was as interested in managing the right-wing headbangers in the Tory party who might be tempted to defect to UKIP as he was in forcing a showdown with Labour.

It was all a bit unnerving. Unsettling. And the strain showed on everyone, especially Ed. He grew increasingly distant and brittle. Just at the moment when he needed to be engaged and show leadership. Where once he had been relaxed and chatty with everyone, he was now withdrawn and monosyllabic. Almost as if he was already living the disaster that he expected to unfold. His conversations with me were now no more than, 'Hi Herbie. Everything OK?' He seldom waited for an answer. It was all perfectly civil, but no more than that.

Then late one Friday afternoon in July, he knocked on the door of my office. It was a hot day, the sun was streaming through the window, and I was curled up on my chair having a quick snooze before sending out the email letting the media know who was on duty for Labour over the weekend.

'Come in,' I said.

Ed pushed open the door and sat down on the sofa next to the window.

'I've been thinking,' he said.

'Yes . . .' This didn't sound promising.

'I want you to be my media person. I mean, dog. Not the one who fends off requests from telly and print. More important than that. I want you to help me sell myself to the country. Because I know I can come across as a bit awkward. Hard to relate to. I want people to be able to trust me. Everyone likes you. You're easy to talk to. Approachable. You have an authenticity that no one else in my inner team has. People feel like they know who you are on first meeting you. What you see is what you get. Maybe it's the fact you come from south London. You've lived a bit. Seen a bit. You have the common touch. Everyone else I know feels anxious leaving Islington.'

'OK,' I said. It would be a challenge and there was no guarantee of success. But it was worth a shot. 'First though, we have to talk about THE THING.'

'What THE THING?'

'Come on, Ed. You know. Everyone in the office knows what THE THING is. Half of them are still suffering from PTSD over it. And everyone's too terrified to talk about it.'

'Ah, that.'

'Yes, ah that. The nightmare few days just before I joined your office when first you had no idea how much a weekly shop cost in a TV interview and then got caught eating a bacon sandwich the wrong way.'

'I'm not sure you're anyone to lecture me on how to eat a bacon sandwich. I've seen your table manners. They leave a lot to be desired.'

'We're not here to talk about me. But as it happens, I can scoff a bacon sarnie in seconds. If you had done that, the public would have loved you. It was more the way you looked like you had never seen a sandwich before and then some bloke grabbing it off you half-eaten.'

'Mmm.'

'These things matter. We've got to change your image. Because most of the media will be hostile and out to make you look silly. Now, that TV interview. Why did you not just say you've been a bit busy recently and Justine has been doing the shopping. Or some other reason for not knowing the cost of the basics. That's the kind of question journos always try out on politicians.'

'I dunno. I just panicked. Besides, we only ever eat sourdough bread? Can you actually get that in Tooting?'

'Yeah, as it happens we can. And focaccia too. Once we've made our way through armed gangs looting all the shops.'

'Seriously?'

'Look we've got a lot of work to do. From now on I'm going to test you on twenty basic food items every week.'

'OK.'

I could sense a crack in his defences. He was listening. Maybe he was ready for more. The real fault line.

'We also need to talk about David. Your brother.'

'What about him?'

'You feel guilty about being leader, don't you? That you somehow stole David's birthright.'

'What if I do?'

'It's holding you back from taking ownership of the job. You don't have to feel bad. There is no law of primogeniture in the Labour Party constitution. David might have felt he had it in the bag but you won the contest fair and square. There was no cheating. Imagine if it had been me or one of my brothers. Now, my mother Hattie – you would have loved her – never got round to telling any of us in what order we were born. Maybe she was doing us a favour. I could be the eldest, I could be the youngest. It really doesn't matter. The fact is that if we'd all been going for the same job, then we'd have all had to live with that. Dog eat dog. Not literally. No hard feelings. May the best dog win.'

'Yeah, you're right. But I can't help feeling bad. David has barely spoken to me since . . .'

'Shit happens in families. I haven't seen any of my siblings since I was eight weeks old. Not even a text. Now they might have gone on to have great lives with far better families than mine. Or they might be miserable. I've no way of knowing. And I have no control over it. So, I just have to accept things how they are. If any of them were to get in touch, I'm sure it would be lovely. But until then, they have to exist as memories. So, I choose to believe they are happy. And you need to do the same with David. When he's ready to reconnect, he will. Maybe he will, maybe he won't. In the meantime, try to live in the present.'

'You're right.'

It would be nice to say that the tension lifted from Ed's body. That he was ready to move on. But that kind of catharsis only comes in books. Let's just say he didn't look quite as haunted as he had earlier on.

I walked across the room, climbed up on to the sofa and put a paw on his shoulder.

'It's going to be OK,' I said. 'We've made a start. Small steps and all that. Now let's wind down for the summer. Take some proper time off away from Westminster. Then we can come back in September and get down to the proper work. Let's try and win this election.'

Chapter 6

It was the most glorious summer holiday. Not that you would have known it from the way John and Jill went on about it. Always moaning about the weather. I mean what did they expect? It was Cornwall after all. They'd been there plenty of times before so they should have known it rains more often than not and that a sunny day is something to be treasured. But for me it was just perfect.

The journey down was a bit of a schlep. Long queues on the A303 as normal with me cramped in the back seat alongside the luggage. You'd have thought they would at least let me have a turn in the front seat. But no. Every time I nudged my nose through the gap between the seats, I got pushed back. It made navigating awfully tricky. I've got a very good memory for places and I like to look out the front window and bark directions.

Once we got there, I could feel myself start to relax. To forget the pressures of Westminster. For a couple of

weeks, I could just be me. Reconnect with my inner dog and forget about trying to make a good impression. Just go for long walks along the cliffs. Run about chasing balls on Constantine beach. Get my feet wet paddling in the sea. I don't like going in any deeper. It's a bit scary. Eat Cornish pasties for lunch. Roll about in the sand. Feel the wind in my fur, pinning back my ears.

The early mornings were heaven. At first light, I would jump off the bed and sneak out to the beach. Hundreds of yards of sand and just me and a handful of insomniacs. After a bit of running around I would just lie down and stare into the sublime. That place where the sky and the sea merge into one. A glimpse of the infinite, where anything seemed possible. Dogs past and dogs present meeting in dogs future. A moment where I felt spiritually connected to the world. Where the temporal momentarily feels eternal.

One of my closest friends, Teasel – I know, what kind of a name is that? – a black labrador, was also there. She had brought her humans, Terry and Anthe, to come and stay as well. Teasel and I go way back. We're almost exactly the same age and we'd been on holiday in Cornwall several times before. She has some strange habits. She likes to talk about old football and cricket matches that she can't possibly have been to and I just sort of nod my head and indulge her. There again, I guess I'm no one to speak. Because I've also got my foibles. I like to read a lot. That summer I reread the Sherlock Holmes short stories. I'm a sucker for a mystery.

Best of all, though, were the smells. You just can't beat the smells of the seaside. The saltiness. The stray corners of sandwiches that have been left behind. The fragrance of the freshly mown golf greens tucked behind the dunes. Barbecued sausages. It was sensory overload. A twenty-four-hour endorphin rush. I've seldom felt more alive. More me.

It was such a change from the day job where the smells were often overpoweringly pungent. It's all right for humans. Their olfactory systems are decidedly third rate so most of the nastiness passes them by. But for us dogs with designer noses, it can get putrid. Charles Dickens had it right when he described London as 'the Big Stink'; that's often how it was around my patch of SW1.

I didn't mind Ed so much. He merely radiated a low-level dose of insecurity that manifested itself as overactive adrenal glands; the smell of a man who was always nervous that he was about to be found out in some way. Even when he had nothing much to be anxious about. Maybe that's the price you pay for thinking you're the right person to lead a country. At some level, your psyche finds you out and your subconscious has a laugh at your own expense.

All that was tolerable. Understandable even. It was the smell of Dan and the dozens of wannabe Dans and Lucys that inhabited Portcullis House that I found unbearable. This was the smell of carelessness. The whiff of insincerity. A cold and clammy aroma. One that was probably undetectable to humans but was toxic to us dogs. It almost had you longing for Lynx Africa. Over-entitled pushy young men and women whose only currency was their own personal gain. They weren't that interested in the policies of the party they worked for. Just what might advance their careers. Other people were only staging posts on their shallow journey to the top.

But I digress. Cornish holidays are also great for the long daytime sleeps. Either curled up behind the windbreak on the beach or stretched out on the kitchen floor with half an eye open for any stray snacks. It was almost the perfect fortnight. Long chats with Teasel and an agreement with the humans that we wouldn't talk politics. The ideal way to unwind. Plenty of laughs, comfortable sofas, a big garden and even bigger skies. Food for the soul.

All too soon, though, it was time to head back to London. Time to re-engage and put on the grown-up doggy face again. It was going to be a tough eight months in the countdown to the election in May. Still, I was looking forward to seeing the new, emotionally connected Ed. To help him learn how to present his best self to the country. Who knows? Get it right and he stood a decent chance of winning the election. Or at least being leader of the largest party. Big mistake on my part, as it turned out. That will teach me to learn to read the room better.

I realised something was wrong on my first day back. I'd had my usual early morning walk on Tooting Common and had then headed straight off to the Tube, getting in to Westminster shortly after 9.30 only to find that Ed had shut himself in his office with Dan. He didn't even pop out to say hello. I didn't think too much of it at first. Maybe there was a mini crisis going on. A member of the shadow cabinet had said something idiotic on the morning media round. Wouldn't be the first time. Certainly wouldn't be the last. So, I just hopped up on to my chair and started idly watching Sky News and checking through my emails.

An hour or so later, Ed eventually appeared. 'How were your hols?' he asked while staring at his phone. This wasn't like him. He normally bothered to make eye contact when speaking to me. Now, it was almost as if he was feeling guilty. I tried not to let it bother me, so I just said that Cornwall had been fine and we had had a good time. Which seemed all he wanted to hear.

For much of the rest of the morning, I just mooched around. Thinking up suggestions for the weekly ideas meeting. The main purpose of which seemed to be for everyone to rubbish anything they hadn't thought of first. While Ed just looked on and said almost nothing. I did have lunch with one of the Lucys – I can't precisely remember which one – a ham sandwich for me and jerk chicken for her. I would have had the same but I can't manage the bones. Then I nipped out to Westminster Square to stretch my legs and have a piss. The parliamentary authorities pride themselves on their inclusivity training, but they haven't yet got as far as providing toilets for dogs. Or for people who identify as dogs. I'm not sure where George Galloway was supposed to go. He identified as a cat. When I first started working for Ed, I had imagined that the indoor trees in Portcullis House were public urinals for me and I climbed up to relieve myself. I didn't do that again. Several policemen with guns appeared and started shouting at me.

'OK, OK,' I said. 'There's no need to shame me in public. It was an easy and honest mistake to make. I mean, why else would someone waste £30K planting a tree indoors if it wasn't to double up as a toilet for us mutts?'

Back in the office, I had a quick snooze in the corner before getting back to work. I cast my eyes over an opinion piece Ed was hoping to place in the *Daily Mail* – for some reason Ed was obsessed with being nice to the *Mail* even though they were almost always beastly to him. I think it's some kind of Labour masochism to always want the approval of the people who treat you the worst – but my heart wasn't in it. I knew something was up.

Just as I was getting ready to go home, Ed came into my room and shut the door. 'We need to talk,' he said. 'I've been thinking . . .' Hmm. That was generally code for Dan had been telling him something.

'Fire away.'

'It's . . . It's just that I've been thinking that maybe it wasn't such a great idea to appoint you as my media person after all.'

'I see,' I said non-committally. 'But how would you know? It's not as if I have actually done anything yet. We haven't even started the work.'

'I know. But . . . I think it's kind of weird for me to have a dog in such a prominent role.'

He did have a point. It was a bit weird. But wasn't that the point? I mean sooner or later a dog had to break through the glass ceiling, and why shouldn't that dog be me? I mean, otherwise all dogs would forever be treated as dogs.

'OK,' I said. 'I get it. But whatever happened to our conversation in the summer? You asked me because out of all humans and canines, I was the best dog for the job. All the others in your office are nice enough, but they either have one eye on their own careers or just tell you what you want to hear. Only I have the necessary emotional intelligence. You can rely on me to tell you the truth. The whole point of me is that I don't lie.' Well, maybe about whether I've climbed up on the sofa. But not about the big things. I'm existentially primed for honesty.

But Ed wasn't having any of it. He had concluded that people found him weird enough without giving them any more ammo by doing something even more weird like giving a top job to a dog. He wanted to go thoroughly mainstream and play it by the book. Even if it would cost him.

'That's fine,' I said. 'It's your call.' What else could I say? He had clearly made up his mind and nothing I was going to say could change it. I suppose I could have stomped off in a huff with my tail between my legs. But the thing is, I liked working for Ed. I believed in what he was doing. He was a nice guy. A good guy. He wasn't the radical he was so often portrayed to be. He was more centre left. Much like me. Most dogs are. We tend to prize fairness above all else. We are all for extending the NHS to include dogs. It isn't right that some hounds are excluded from veterinary treatments because their humans can't afford to pay the bills. I have met some dogs on the common who haven't even had their basic injections. That isn't right.

'Don't worry,' Ed said. 'I still want your input. You're still an important member of my team. Just maybe take a bit more of a back seat. Let Dan and Ben take the lead on the media stuff.'

Ed ruffled my fur and tickled me under the chin. It was all I could do not to roll on my back. Thankfully, I kept my dignity. We were friends again. I would just have to accept my place near the bottom of the pack.

* * *

The next few weeks were frantic as we prepared for the Labour Party conference in Manchester. John and Jill got decidedly short-changed on the morning walks. The last one before the election, so Ed was determined to make a good impression. I was flattered to be assigned to the team in charge of writing his speech. His big pitch to the voters. A chance to reassure them he could be trusted not to do anything daft. That he wasn't about to go and bankrupt the country. Well, not deliberately.

At one of the first planning meetings, Ed announced that he had had a brilliant idea. A game-changer. So, why did I have this sinking feeling?

'I'm going to do a David Cameron,' he said. 'Remember how in 2007 he wowed the Conservative Party conference by giving his entire speech without autocue? Well, I'm going to do the same. The country is going to love it.'

'Well, I love it,' Dan exclaimed.

'Me too. You're going to knock them dead,' said Lucy. Lucy Two. By now I had learned to differentiate between her and Lucy One.

Great. It was down to me to be the killjoy. As per.

'It's not a macho contest,' I said. Though it clearly was. 'What does giving a speech without help actually prove? Other than you've got a good memory. Like an actor. Surely, it's the message that's the most important thing. No one will really care how you delivered the speech a couple of days afterwards. Unless you mess up. Then the messing up is all they will remember. So why bother with the stress?'

But Ed, Dan and Lucy Two were all determined. This was going to shift the dial. Now it was down to us to try and think of a way to make it as easy as possible for Ed to memorise a speech that was due to clock in at about fifty minutes. Lucy One suggested meditation and an isolation tank. I rather thought that something more practical was called for.

'How about we divide the speech into sections?' I suggested. 'The economy, the NHS, schools etc. And then we write in some easy-to-remember links. Like meetings with fictitious people that would tee up each section. So, Elena from Eltham would be the way into education.'

It wasn't much, but amazingly, everyone seemed to think that was the best option. Mainly because no one was able to think of anything better. The scale of the undertaking was slowly becoming apparent, but Ed insisted he was up for the challenge.

I can't say I really enjoyed much of the conference. Far too many people for my liking and being quite small I was constantly having to make sure I didn't accidentally get trampled on. And some of the security guards refused to admit me to events even though I had my conference pass tied round my neck. One even tried to keep me out of my room in the Midland Hotel. I thought we should have been well past that sort of discrimination in 2014. I guess these battles need to be fought and refought.

On the Tuesday, the day of Ed's speech, I was probably as nervous as he was. I couldn't even eat my breakfast. I just wanted the whole thing to be over. 'You're going to be fine,' I whispered to Ed, as he went to take his place on the stage. Then I settled down to watch it on the TV.

'We're Betta Togetha. Togetha we are Betta,' Ed began. He always dropped his consonants when he was anxious. Thought he sounded more like Tony Blair. He never quite got that what voters really want is integrity. Someone who will do what they say they will. Not someone trying to sound like a man of the people. He waited for applause, which eventually came.

'But don't just take it from me. Here's Elizabeth. Elizabeth is an apprentice. I met her yesterday. She's right here behind me somewhere. Where are you, Elizabeth? Ah, there you are. Stand up, please, Elizabeth. Friends, give Elizabeth a round of applause for standing up. Thank you, Elizabeth.

'Now here's the thing. The otha day I was in the park. Primrose Hill. An' I got talkin' to two ordinree women. Their names were Beatrice and Helen. They were hopin' to meet Benedict Cumberbatch but they got me instead. Some girls have all the luck!'

No one laughed. I knew people wouldn't find that funny. I had told him to cut that gag.

'And what Beatrice and Helen said to me was that this Tory government is makin' it harda and harda to complete a doctorate on Victorian women's bodies in art. And that really resonated with me. So for them I promise to raise the minimum wage.

'Then there's Gareth. Now here's the thing. Gareth needs an operation to help him stay awake when I am talkin'. But Gareth can't have that operation because the NHS where Gareth lives is broken. And I wants to fix that for Gareth. But I can't do that on my own. With your help, friends, I can. Which is why I is going to introduce a mansion tax and impose a windfall tax on tobacco companies.

'You know somethin? I don't just think we can be Betta Togetha. I think we can be Gr8a Togetha. Because we are more than one nation. Last week, I was in Scotland. You heard. Scotland, that place a long way away from London near Cornwall. In Scotland, I met a man called Alex. Now Alex started shouting at me, "What the hell has Westminster ever done for me?" An' you know, I told him we were Gr8a Togetha.

'This won't be easy. Which is why I make this pledge here to you, today, at this time, that I will also solve the Middle East crisis. So, here's the thing, friends. I want a faira, betta Britain. With your help, I can do it. Thank you.'

The shadow cabinet – bless them – rose as one as soon as Ed finished speaking to give him a standing ovation. And thankfully most of the rest of the conference hall followed suit. It hadn't been a great speech – large sections of it had been instantly forgettable: not my bits, I hasten to add – but it looked as if Ed had just about got away with it.

Something was niggling me, though. I checked the time. Somehow Ed had cracked through the thing in just under forty minutes. Then it hit me. He had left out a whole chunk. He had completely forgotten how he had met Debby from Dulwich, which was his cue to talk about the deficit. Now that omission would become the entire story. No one would care about any of the things he had said. Once they had read the speech he was meant to have given, which would have been emailed round to all the lobby journalists, everyone would merely focus on what he hadn't said. The right-wing press, in particular, would claim this was a Freudian slip. Proof that Labour couldn't be trusted with the economy. It was a disaster of Ed's own making. One that could have been easily avoided.

Ed was devastated when he realised what he had done. We all tried to cheer him up and said it wasn't that serious. But it was really. The voters might forget about it quite soon – assuming they'd even been listening in the first place – but the media and the party apparatchiks . . . It would be just another thing, another misstep, with which to beat Ed. A sign that he wasn't a serious politician for serious times. Fair to say, it was a rather silent trip back to London the following day.

* * *

I guess it was only a matter of time. The inevitable post-mortem into what had gone wrong in Manchester kicked off the following week when Ed summoned his whole team in for a debrief. Oddly, the question of whose idiotic idea it had been to do the entire speech from memory was never raised. That's because it had clearly been Ed and Dan's and they weren't in the mood to take any of the blame. I suppose I could have pointed this out but I bottled it. This was definitely one of those meetings where the messenger was first in line to get shot.

Not that my silence did me much good. The hunt was on for a fall guy and I was that guy. It's always easiest to pick on the dog. People use us as a displacement triangulation point. Rather than express their anger with each other, they avoid confrontation by taking it out on us. Even though we are perfectly capable of talking back. So, yours truly got it in the neck. It had been this pooch that had screwed the pooch apparently. Somehow, everything got distorted, rewritten into a new narrative. The simple memory aids that I had suggested be inserted into the speech had not just failed, they had actually made Ed's life more difficult. It got forgotten that everyone had thought they were a good idea at the time. Now everything was my fault.

'I always knew it was asking for trouble employing a dog,' said Dan. He managed to lace the word 'dog' with contempt. No one stopped to ask themselves the obvious counterfactual. Maybe, without my help, Ed would have forgotten even more of his speech. Let's hear it for Beatrice and Helen. Maybe Ed's memory wasn't quite as good as he had hoped. Maybe, if he hadn't been so focused on remembering his words, he might have been able to stop to breathe and engage more naturally with his audience and he wouldn't have sounded so frenetic. The autocue is the speaker's friend. No one would have thought worse of him for using one.

But we were where we were and everyone had decided I was the problem. So, I was now effectively side-lined. Nothing was ever made explicit, and Ed did mumble something about 'no one is blaming Herbie' and the buck stopping with him, but no one appeared to be listening that hard. The mission was complete. A scapegoat had been found and everyone else involved in the speech-writing process was off the hook.

All of which made the following months rather dispiriting. I wasn't ostracised exactly – I was still invited to meetings and went along to lunches in the canteen – but I no longer felt that involved with the day-to-day running of the operation. My contributions were tolerated rather than valued and seldom acted on. Not great for a dog's self-worth. Some dogs might get a kick out of chasing balls. My mate Billy, sadly long since dead, once savaged a sheep: his humans, Jane and Stephen, had a lot of explaining to do with the farmer. But I wanted more out of life than that. My pleasures were more cerebral.

You might ask why I didn't just leave. Say, 'Thanks but no thanks,' to Ed. Be grateful for the opportunity. To be fair, Ed was the first politician I knew to hire a dog, unless you count David Blunkett, but guide dogs are a different category. Perhaps I should just have acknowledged that sometimes these things don't work out. But I didn't want to give up. Partly because of the message it would have sent to other mutts. It would have looked like dogs just couldn't hack it in the world of politics and it would be ages before a party leader was brave enough to employ a dog again. But, also, because I actually really liked Ed. There was a vulnerability to him that touched something in my soul. I also thought there was a genuine possibility he would be the next prime minister. The opinion polls were still very tight and if there was to be a hung parliament, I reckoned Labour would be best placed to form a coalition, as no opposition party would ever trust the Tories in government again after the way they had screwed over the Lib Dems. So I wanted to be there for Ed's triumph. And also to be the first dog to work in Downing Street. As opposed to George Osborne's dog, Lola, who just sat around in Number 11 doing nothing all day. Rumour had it on the dog grapevine that she was bored out of her mind.

So, I hung around. Just putting one paw in front of the other. Making sure I was one of the first in and the last to leave – Jill and John were a bit pissed off at that. They reckoned I should be spending more time with them, doing more about the home. Instead I concentrated on being assertive rather than pushy: always quick to acknowledge when someone else had done something well. The consummate professional working dog, in fact. Trying to help out with the weekly preparations for PMQs. David Cameron was a tricky opponent. Slippery even. It felt like it ought to be easy to do him some political damage. After all, the

Tories were having a tough time with their Eurosceptics creating trouble, two MPs defecting to UKIP and several more threatening to do so. But Dave was evasive. Hard to pin down. And most of Ed's best lines failed to land. It was incredibly annoying. Worst of all, you could sense some of the Labour MPs were getting frustrated with Ed. But I'm not sure what more he could have done.

Christmas was short and sweet. Ten days RnR in Tooting. Walks with Anna and Robbie who were also back home – they seemed quite pleased with the branded chocolates I had bought from the House of Commons shop – but mainly just sleeping. You sometimes don't realise how tired you are until you get a chance to sleep. And I kept my phone switched off. If anything important was kicking off, I didn't want to know. If they really wanted me, they knew where to find me.

Then back to the hard grind. Those last four months before the general election were brutal. Everyone was on edge and there were endless meetings with shadow cabinet ministers lobbying for more spending commitments for their departments to be included in the manifesto.

And of course there were the usual wobbles. Dan and Lucy One were constantly on the phone to the *Daily Mail* asking them not to call Ed 'Red Ed'. But predictably that only encouraged the *Mail* to do it more, as they could see it had cut through. I thought it was quite funny. The more Ed tried to look like a non-threatening centrist, the more hysterical the right-wing media became. To me, it was a sign he was being taken seriously.

Then there was Kitchengate. Happy to say this one wasn't on me. My paw prints weren't on this one. Ed had become paranoid about people thinking his kitchen was too posh and he encouraged the BBC to film an 'at home' with him and his wife, Justine, in the small galley kitchenette they seldom used. Sure enough, an old friend of Ed's, Jenni Russell, helpfully later told everyone that of course he had a bigger kitchen and then everyone piled in. Ed's desperate attempt to conform to some mythical archetype of a 'man of the people' was his undoing again. Now everyone assumed he must be mega well-off. Which of course he was. Houses in that part of north London don't come cheap.

But come the election campaign proper, Ed was a changed man. Less uncertain than he had been. Confident in himself and what he had to say. I spent most of the weeks at Labour head office in London, trying to come up with attack lines in response to the Tories' manifesto and wasn't part of the team preparing Ed for the four televised leaders' debates. Just as well, I guess, as Cameron was perceived to have shaded them. So no comebacks on me.

Still, I was pleased to be invited up to Manchester for the launch of Labour's manifesto. The catchily titled, 'Better Plan, Better Future'. I know, I know. I didn't write that bit. I'm not sure if it was the better-than-expected opinion polls, the all-too-visible Tory jitters or the *Daily Mail* plan to portray Ed as something of a superstud that had spectacularly backfired, but Ed was now on cracking form. Clearly being thought of as a serial shagger suited him down to the ground. Made him look much more human. Less geeky.

Ed strode into the studio space next door to the Coronation Street set to a standing ovation and never looked back. 'Thank you, thank you,' he said repeatedly. And he hadn't even yet done anything. This was to be a radical manifesto, he went on. Radical because he wasn't making any promises that weren't properly costed and funded. That was my suggestion. You wouldn't go to a bank manager asking for a loan without submitting a budget. And asking to run the country should be no different. To me, it seemed like basic stuff. Politics 101. No dog would turn up for something without the means to pay for it. But apparently this was a groundbreaking vision in politics. Anyway, come the end, Ed was virtually liquid. Pouring himself into the eyes of every member of the audience, into the lens of every TV camera. All the while sounding like some latter-day Barry White crooning, 'Trust me, Trust me'. The chemistry was almost sexual.

It all seemed to be going so well. Too well. Then on the Sunday morning before the election, while I was dozing on the sofa having a lie-in, I got a text from Ben. 'Turn on the TV. Now.' I scampered to the living room, flicked the remote and there was Ed, somewhere on the south coast, standing in front of a giant stone tablet with six pledges on it, all of them third-rate promises dreamed up in a focus group. Things like, 'An NHS with Time to Care' and 'A Country where the Next Generation can do Better than the Last'. I mean, that's hardly brilliant communications. Who wouldn't want that? What the fuck would archaeologists make of it if they came across it in a thousand years' time. They'd have to conclude we were a civilisation of half-wits. Still, at least there were only six and not the full ten. Imagine if Moses had come down from Mount Sinai with these mindless new-age affirmations. 'Thou must try not to kill but we accept that accidents do happen.' The whole history of the Old Testament would have to be rewritten.

But Ed clearly thought this was a game-changer. The clincher in the race to Number 10. He was even promising to erect this monstrosity in the Downing Street garden. I texted Ben, asking which moron had dreamt this one up. He didn't know. Though he assumed Dan must have been in on it. No one was going to own up to this one. It was more than an embarrassment; it was a disaster. It would become the focus of the last few days of the campaign. Just when Ed was beginning to be thought of as a credible option. I switched off the TV and went back to the sofa. I couldn't think of anything else to do.

On the night of the election, I made my way to Labour HQ to watch the results. One of the more dismal nights of my life. In the days since the Edstone fiasco I had allowed myself to hope again. That people would want a change from austerity and a party fighting with itself over Europe. That they would see that Ed was fundamentally a decent guy. At 10 pm, I just felt despair. Far from being the hung parliament that everyone expected, the Tories were predicted to win an outright majority. At first, I dared to think that the polls might be wrong but the first results proved otherwise. Come the morning, David Cameron had won 330 seats, while Labour won twenty-six fewer than in 2010.

We all knew what was going to happen next. The following morning, Ed called a press conference and announced he was resigning as leader of the Labour Party. Afterwards he was in tears, as was almost everyone else in his team. Apart from me. I don't do crying. That's not me being hard-hearted. I just can't. It doesn't mean I don't feel. Sometimes I think I care more than humans. We all knew it was the end for us, too. No Ed, no jobs for the boys and girls. Or for the dog. So I mooched back to the office in Westminster to collect my things and then went home.

Politics can be brutal. One minute you think you are headed for Downing Street, the next you are out on your ear. I felt desperate. Washed up at three years old.

Chapter 7

One thing they never tell you about losing your job. Your phone goes dead. It's something that never occurs to you when you are in work. I certainly didn't. The endless texts from Dan reminding me to go to meetings I hadn't actually forgotten about because I am not a dopey halfwit, whatever John might say when I'm dawdling on a walk. Dawdling is my thinking time. Where the unconscious becomes conscious.

The humblebrags, masquerading as important memos, from other members of the team who wanted to let you know that Ed was very grateful for what they had been doing. The alerts that invariably told you something you already knew because we all had the rolling news channels on in the background. What unites almost everyone in Westminster – politicians, advisers and hacks – is that we were all fantastically needy, even us dogs. Could never get too much

attention. It's surprising how few of us were aware of it though.

On average only about one in ten texts were really necessary. The actual phone calls were something of a mixed bag. Either a lobby reporter wanting to know something or Dan shouting at you for something that was probably his fault. I learned to screen my calls quite carefully.

But once I was back in Tooting, all of this stopped. After Ed had said his tearful goodbyes to us, thanking us for all our hard work and saying that no one could have done more, I didn't hear from him again for many years. Not that I blamed him. He was locked in a private grief, his political ambitions in tatters. He had had one shot at the prize and wouldn't get another. Maybe he was even wondering whether his brother might have won the election. The comparisons were bound to be made. And all the while, he would have to put on a show for everyone in Westminster. Keep the artificial smile flying. It's almost a tradition for senior politicians to pretend that they are relaxed about their fall from office. 'Just the nature of the job,' they say. Almost as a joke. But inside they are dying. No wonder so many weird people are attracted to politics.

Lucy Two did say that she was going to organise reunion drinks in a month or so for all those of us who had worked in Ed's office. Maybe then we'd all be able to laugh about it. Right now it was too raw. But those drinks never happened. Maybe she had just mentioned the idea to make us all feel better at the time and had never intended to do anything about it. Or perhaps, when the time came, she just couldn't face it. Too much like reopening old wounds. Possibly everyone had moved on. It was a ruthless business and all the team were in it for the long haul. Right now, they would all be looking for another Labour MP to attach themselves to. There again, maybe the drinks did go ahead and I wasn't invited. Time to ditch the dog. There had always been one or two who had made no secret of their ambivalence about working alongside a mutt. Oxbridge hadn't prepared them for that. Well, think about it from my point of view. Having to work with people like them. Mediocre minds and mediocre talent. Not that I'm bitter.

For ages, I would just stare at my phone, willing it to ring or ping. I just couldn't break the habit. Sometimes I would spend the best part of an hour doom-scrolling my way through Twitter. As if all this could make something happen. It didn't, of course. Most of the calls I did get were from Jill, who was working upstairs in her office, asking if I was ready to take her out for a walk. Hell, why not? I wasn't exactly busy.

My mind was scrambled. I dare say most of the rest of the team barely gave Ed another thought. Had concluded that Ed was the problem, not them, and had moved on to the next shiny thing. But not me. We dogs tend to have an overdeveloped superego. Sure there are some psychopaths, dogs who like nothing more than threatening other dogs and humans, but most of us are genuinely good-natured. Well disposed to the world. If someone or some dog is friendly towards us, then we are friendly back. Hostility gets to be so enervating. It could be that I'm lazy, but I don't have the energy to be on my guard the whole time.

So part of me couldn't help tormenting myself. Replaying episodes from my year in Westminster, worrying I had let Ed down. Perhaps if I'd structured the links in his conference speech differently, he wouldn't have missed out a large chunk. If I had been a bit more forceful . . . As a dog, you have to be twice as good as a woman to get on in life. To get your achievements recognised. So, there was always the possibility I hadn't made the grade. That another dog might have won the general election for Ed.

Then there was the shame. That's always a killer. A knife wound to one's self-worth. The feeling that I had very publicly failed. It would be on my CV forever that I had been part of the team that had delivered a worse-than-expected result at the general election. In my mind, I could picture other dogs and humans laughing at me behind my back when I was out on the streets. 'Oh, there goes Herbie! Thought he could genuinely hack it in the human world. What a loser. Twat.' The most humiliating thing was that part of me felt like they had a point. I was just another mutt with ideas above his station.

All in all, I wasn't much fun to be around. I was withdrawn. Depressed even. Though I was never tempted to try any of John's psychiatric meds. I definitely wasn't that fucked up. Most days, I would just sit and stare out the kitchen window or snooze on the bed. Not even a walk cheered me up that much. The smells just didn't feel quite right and the landscape felt two-dimensional, fading into grey. My sense of fun had gone. I could scarcely even be bothered to fetch a stick. That bad.

Help came from an unexpected quarter. I was out on the common and we were walking at an extra slow dawdle. Not my fault for once. This was entirely down to John, who was on crutches. The moron had only gone and had a stick tattooed on the other arm to the one with me on it. Except he had forgotten he was prone to infections, as he had had one knee replaced years earlier. The knee duly swelled up to twice its normal size and he needed major surgery and six weeks of intravenous antibiotics to save his leg. Talk about half-witted self-destruction. And the tattoo looked like it had been drawn by a five-year-old. Still, I got brownie points for dozing next to him on the bed.

Anyway, we were at the cafe where John liked to stop for a coffee. So, I was free to wander around and see if I could find any friends or hoover up any stray chips or bits of sandwich that had fallen on the ground. Hidden out of sight behind some brambles, I came upon a group of dogs sitting in a circle. Curious to know what was going on, I approached the large, golden dog who appeared to be in charge.

'Hi,' she said. 'My name's Lottie.'

'I'm Herbert Hound.'

'We only do first names here. Though we might also add the first letter of your surname if there's already more than one person in the fellowship with your first name. So you would be Herbert H.'

'What do you mean by fellowship?'

'This is Canines Anonymous. A twelve-step programme. We meet here three times a week to talk about what's on our minds and to come to terms with our different addictions and personality disorders. You're very welcome to stay and join us. Just try to listen for the similarities, not the differences.'

Ordinarily, I would have been tempted to move on. To be the outsider looking in. Keeping my problems to myself. But something about Lottie's openness and fragility touched me. After all, it wasn't as if my life was exactly sunshine and roses at that moment. What did I have to lose?

I shuffled into the circle in between a scary-looking Alsatian and an elderly dachshund who gave me a nice smile. The meeting began with Lottie welcoming everyone and inviting a Jack Russell cross to read something called the Steps. 'We came to believe we were powerless over our canine addictions and that our lives had become unmanageable.' It was a lot to take in.

Next up, Lottie handed over the meeting to the scary-looking Alsatian. 'My name's Ken and I'm compulsive,' he began.

'Hi Ken,' everyone replied. Except me.

Ken then told his story. He had been separated from his mother soon after birth and had then been abandoned by his first humans and left to fend for himself on the street for a few weeks. A dog rescue charity took him in and he was locked up in the pound because no one seemed to want him. He was finally rehomed with a middle-aged couple of humans, but he had been unable to settle. Even though his humans went out of their way to shower him with love and treats, Ken could only react with aggression.

'I just couldn't help myself,' he said. 'I really wanted their love and affection but I just wouldn't allow myself to feel it. I couldn't allow humans into my life after the way I had been let down by them in the past. It tore me apart, rejecting the thing I craved. Then I realised that it was me who had to change. Not my humans, nor my circumstances. It was me who had to stop the self-sabotage. And it was at that point, my rock bottom, that another dog introduced me to CA. That was two years ago and now, thanks to the fellowship, my life is a lot better. I still have my moments but most evenings I am happy lying curled up next to the sofa as my humans watch TV.'

This all sounded a bit hardcore to me. My life hadn't been anywhere near as traumatic as Ken's. I felt that maybe I was here under false pretences. But then I remembered Lottie's advice. Similarities not differences. And while I couldn't relate to all the experiences, I could identify with some of the feelings. That sense of complete hopelessness. That feeling of being out of my depth. A dog in a world mainly inhabited by humans who could only see us as pets or as a menace. Not as beings in our own right. Just animals refracted through the human experience. Also, that feeling I was often my own worst enemy. Often on the defensive, scrabbling for traces of self-worth. I wanted to change that and I could only do it by changing my behaviours.

Most of the rest of the meeting consisted of others sharing their own experience, strength and hope. Some had been coming to this meeting for years, others for a few months. Many were just like me. Living with lovely humans, but with an underlying chaos that made their lives unnecessarily difficult. Compulsive eating, stealing and hiding shoes, running away and pretending to be deaf. Things that we dogs so often like to call playful but which really aren't that clever. Then there were those who were compulsively helpful to humans. Putting their own needs second. None of this was about trying to make us the best dog for humans. It was all about being the best dogs we could be for ourselves. A less complicated, more honest way of living.

A few minutes before the end of the meeting, Lottie interrupted proceedings. 'This is the time we reserve for newcomers and dogs who find it difficult to share,' she said. 'Could other dogs respect this, please?' There was a lengthy pause that extended into a definite silence. I looked up and could feel everyone's eyes looking at me. This was my time. No hiding place.

'Er . . . I'm Herbie and I'm compulsive.'

'Hi Herbie.'

'Um . . . I'm not sure really what to say . . .' I mumbled. It was most unlike me to be lost for words. 'I wasn't expecting to be here or anything. But I am really glad I came. To tell you the truth, I've been feeling a bit lost recently. Overwhelmed by my feelings and acting out. So, I really needed this. That's all I can say for now. Thank you.'

There were a few woofs of approval and then Lottie asked us all to hold paws and recite the serenity prayer. I had no idea what she was talking about so just listened. 'Dog grant me the serenity to accept the things I cannot change, the courage to change the things I can and the wisdom to know the difference.'

'Keep coming back. It works if you work it,' everyone barked. With that we were done. Most dogs strolled off. Things to do. Places to go. Lottie stayed behind to chat to me. Told me it was lovely I had stayed to the end – some newcomers can't hack it and leave in the middle – and hoped I would come again. She even gave me her mobile number in case I wanted someone to chat to.

'Herbie!' That was John calling. Time to go home.

'Don't worry,' I said to Lottie. 'I will be back.'

And I did go back. Not immediately, but several weeks later. Something had registered in my subconscious that this was the safe place I needed. What's more, I've been going to meetings on and off for the past nine years. Not as often as some but regularly enough for me. I guess you could call me a semi-detached old-timer. But it's been a lifeline and I have made many close friends there. I've also introduced several younger dogs to CA over the years. Billy, whom I've mentioned earlier, was a shoo-in. Savaging sheep is a shortcut to a farmer taking a pot shot at you. Not clever. Joey too, whom you've also met. From the outside he looks totally harmless. A sweet-faced cavalier King Charles spaniel. But he sure did have attitude problems. I christened him the Delinquent as he couldn't help himself attacking other dogs. Then there was Pippin, another cockapoo. She is the only dog I know who's had open-heart surgery. But no sooner was she back home than she broke into the medicine cabinet and overdosed on her heart meds. Makes me look normal.

I don't want to get too misty-eyed over meetings. While they were usually good soul food, they could also be annoying. I mean, what else would you expect from a bunch of dogs who all admitted to being mentally unwell. Why else would they come to CA? There was a hardcore group of mutts who took a dim view of anyone they thought wasn't taking the programme seriously enough. Weren't working the steps properly. They specialised in passive aggression. Their usual tactic was to wait until some unfortunate had shared and then chip in with, 'Thank you for that. I could identify with everything you said.' Only to then go on to say how they had dealt with the same issues completely differently. And, by implication, much better. These were the self-proclaimed spiritual giants.

There were also moments of high comedy. A few dogs were natural storytellers. Could narrate their struggles with both humility and humour. I could have listened to them for hours. Then came the unintentional laughs. Some I will never forget. There was this obese, potty-mouthed Staffy who couldn't stop himself wolfing down everything in sight. For obvious reasons, we all called him Fat Ben. Everyone had a nickname in the early days of CA and fat shaming wasn't a thing back then. He brought the house down by beginning one of his shares by saying, 'I'm Ben and I'm a fat fuck. I can say that today because, thanks to the programme, I have self-acceptance.' There was also Paul who always seemed to start talking halfway into a thought. Usually with the word 'that'. It was one way of getting us all to listen, I suppose, as we all had to mentally fill in the blanks for it to make any sense whatsoever. Happy days.

But however deconstructed a meeting became, you could almost always be guaranteed to hear something you needed to hear. It was just a matter of keeping your ears and heart open. And just occasionally something very special, almost, mystical would happen. Like the time the Tooting meeting decided to break with convention and invite a guest speaker. Step forward, Leonard Cohen, the only human ever to have been asked to give a talk at a meeting of CA. We chose him because we felt he was one of the few humans to exist on the higher level of consciousness where we dogs operate. He understood us, spoke to us through his poetry and song. And Lenny accepted our invitation as he was in the UK on a concert tour. That was quite the occasion. The golden voice that was almost a growl. He seemed pleased to be accepted as an honorary dog.

Yet this still wasn't quite enough for me. CA was the ideal launchpad for improving my mental health but it only promised freedom from acting out on your compulsions and I wanted more than that. I needed to resolve some of my childhood trauma, to be able to stop making the same mistakes over and over again. Or if I couldn't manage that to at least understand why I was making the same mistakes again and again. This didn't sit well with some dogs in CA. They felt that dogs like me who tended to go on and on about how difficult they were still finding life were a bad advert for the programme. New dogs coming to CA would be put off by hearing dogs like me, who had been around the brambles for a while, talking like this, was how they put it. They thought I'd be better off working the steps a bit harder and then all my difficult feelings would melt away.

It didn't feel quite right to me. I thought new dogs might gain from seeing others like me who were still struggling. Reality in real time. After all, life doesn't stop coming at you just because you've got clean from your compulsions. It just comes at you in different ways. But I didn't want to rock the boat. So, I thought the time had come to try my paw at therapy.

This was easier said than done. As you might imagine, it was hard to find a therapist. It's hard enough for a human – all the good therapists are generally busy and there's no knowing if you will click with one another if one does have a free hour. So, think how difficult it is to find one who has experience of working with dogs. You don't want a shrink who is permanently trying to turn you into a human.

Not surprisingly, my first venture into the therapy world was not a success. So much so, I can't even remember her name. Then, I doubt she could remember mine either. I don't think we made that much impression on one another. In theory, she should have been ideal. A blank canvas onto which I could project my hopes and fears and have them reinterpreted back to me. But it never really worked out as she never really said very much to me at all. Except to tell me when my fifty minutes were up. And, while I learned a great deal about the experience of not feeling heard, this wasn't what I had come here for. The ending, which came after just a few months, was a snapshot of our entire relationship. I turned up for a session and rang the doorbell. No one answered, so I just trooped off back to the Tube. And that was that. I never did find out why no one buzzed to let me in and I am certain I rang the right bell as I pressed it several times. So, the relationship ended as it had begun in amiable indifference. At least no one got hurt. We hadn't been close enough for that.

My next therapist, Caroline, was a whole new ball game. Albeit another total disaster. I sure do pick them. If you didn't need therapy before seeing Caroline, you sure as hell would need it afterwards. Weirdly, she had come recommended by someone I trusted. Ruby, the Westie, a fellow Spurs obsessive. Caroline must have had something going for her, I suppose. It's just that we never seemed to really hit it off. The closer I felt I was getting to her the more distant she felt. A connection that was forever out of reach. Though maybe that says more about me than her. I dunno. I don't find it that hard to make relationships in the human world. I get along just fine with Jill, John, Anna and Robbie.

It didn't help that Caroline lived at the other end of the Northern line to Tooting Bec and it took over an hour to get to each session. This seemed to give Caroline a perverse sense of satisfaction. In her perfectly measured, pedantic monotone, she would insist that the physical distance between us was a sign of how much I was committed to getting mentally well. Who knows, if I had lived in Brighton, maybe I would have got a pat on the back each session. Metaphorically speaking, of course.

Caroline lived in a house that had an enormous crack down the outside front wall and was situated at the very end of a cul-de-sac. Funnily enough, these two details were the only ones to escape a symbolic interpretation throughout our therapeutic relationship. No matter how often I brought them up to annoy her. The consulting room, as she insisted on calling it, was little more than a shed attached to the side of the house, which was painted in a sickly shade of lilac and had a few rugs with eastern motifs – very Carl Jung – hanging on the walls. And along one side of the room there was a couch on which I stretched out while she sat behind me and waited for me to speak.

At least one session in five, this would mean me starting with an apology for being late. Trying to time my arrival so that I was not hideously early or late was a near impossibility when you're trying to second-guess the problems on the public transport network and the journey involves two buses and a change on the Tube at Kennington. All of which was my fault somehow.

'I think you're late because part of you doesn't want to be here,' Caroline would invariably say. Whereupon I would reply that my powers as a dog didn't, as far as I knew, extend to creating engineering works on the Tube tracks or traffic jams in Colindale. If only my psyche were that powerful. I might then have been able to help Ed win the 2015 general election. But Caroline wouldn't have it any other way. We weren't there for the obvious, the mundane. To everything there was a psychological meaning. We were in a *World of Interiors*.

Much as I hate to admit it, Caroline may have had a point. Not about the trains and the buses. I'm never going to take responsibility for their defects. I know a lot is my fault, but not that. But she was right that part of me didn't want to be in therapy with her. It was just I had no idea – no benchmark – for what a good therapy would look like. This wasn't the relationship I had imagined. Was this part of the natural process, the journey, towards enlightenment or was I going round and round in circles? There was only one way to find out.

'You seem to be stuck,' Caroline observed. Mmm. You could say that. 'Maybe what you need is to increase your sessions to twice a week.' What? Do battle with the Tube and buses twice as often? Be told that I don't want to be here more frequently? Feel even more dislocated and dissociated, like some latter-day Flying Dutchman? Of course, that was exactly what I wanted. I agreed on the spot.

There's no doubt that the extra session a week made a difference. Just not necessarily for the better. It certainly made things a bit more intense. And weirder. First Caroline seemed hell-bent on annoying me. Time and again, she would interject with comments such as, 'I think you're trying to tell me that you're very angry with me.' Now, sometimes I was pissed off with her, sometimes I was mildly irritated by her and sometimes I had no real feelings about her at all at that point in the session. But she would never let go. Certain I was hanging on to some long-repressed pain from my puppyhood that was being played out in that particular moment.

Which felt like a cheap shot. Of course I had problems with my mum but they were a separate issue. I didn't want them dragged into an argument with Caroline that had begun with me being late. Needless to say, though, by the time we were twenty minutes into the session, I was properly angry with Caroline. I was angry she had made me angry. Something that seemed to occasion her great pleasure as she never failed to remark she had been right all along. She didn't buy my argument that what I was mostly angry about was that my session had been hijacked by her and I had just spent £50 not talking about the things I wanted to talk about.

Things also got a bit embarrassing soon after when Caroline remarked, 'Are you trying to say that you find me attractive?' I was horrified. The idea had never occurred to me. I mean, she was a human and I was a dog. Did she think I was some kind of perve dog? I had become quite attached to her, in the masochistic way some patients do. A variation of Stockholm syndrome. But nowhere close to the feelings I had for Jill and John. But all this was strictly platonic. I can assure you at no point did I ever fancy Caroline. I've had my crushes in my time – some of them unrequited – but I can assure you they have all been for other dogs. I am basically a CIS male. Though I have been known to sniff the bums of other dogs when I get carried away. That's just normal in the canine world. Not that Caroline ever quite got that. But look, I'm not going to quibble. Put me down as bi-curious if you must.

Caroline was insistent I was in denial. The more I said I didn't fancy her, the more she said I did. In the end I had to tell her to keep her transference to herself. She did protest too much. Perhaps she fancied me. Not a thought I like to dwell on. Anyway, just as I felt we were hitting a dead end in the therapy – we seemed to disagree on everything – she announced that we were only now getting to the heart of it. And what would seal the deal was if I now increased my therapy to four sessions a week. Hell, it was almost like she was asking me to move in with her. Perhaps she did weekend rates. At this point, I walked away from Caroline. I'm still not sure if that's the bravest or the most stupid thing I've ever done.

I was tempted to give therapy a miss after that. Perhaps it was asking too much for a trained psychotherapist to really understand the dog mind. To make the quantum leap in consciousness. But then I got a call from Liz, a shrink I'd made contact with before but who had had no free time in her week to see me. One of her patients had left, she said, and she could now accommodate me if I was still interested. I was torn between not wanting to put myself through the emotional upheaval all over again and curiosity. Curiosity won. After all, the worst had already happened.

It turned out to be a good call. Liz seemed to get me right from the off. She also had a good sense of humour, which helped. Her opening line was, 'So I see you're a dog. I've never had a patient who is a dog before.'

'Well, I've never had a therapist who was a dog either,' I replied. 'But let's see if we can make this work. Let's get this straight. I am a dog's dog. I am not a dog who identifies as a man. Nor am I a man who identifies as a dog. I am a dog who identifies as a dog. No need for you to worry about my pronouns. I am a dog with dog needs.'

And Liz was OK with that. There was no couch, we just sat opposite each other. Me on the floor – I was happiest there – she in her chair and we just talked. About how I regretted not having a strong male role model in my life. Much like every dog I knew. Why do male dogs make such crap parents? About how my mother let me go at just eight weeks old. Couldn't we even have had six months together? That would have been something. I miss my mum every day. I try to suppress it as there's not much point in dwelling on it and I don't want to upset Jill and John, but it's always there at the back of my mind. I know Hattie didn't have much say in it but couldn't she have fought a little harder to keep me? Was I not worth more than a sad, resigned backward glance?

It's taken time but I hope I have now reached a point of acceptance. Which is not to diminish the loss, but to see my parents for what they were. They weren't bad dogs. They were two emotionally damaged individuals trying to do their best. Dogs who couldn't escape the cultural mores of their generation. So, they just passed the damage on, aided and abetted by humans for whom it was normal to see dogs as just pets. Only there for humans' comfort and entertainment. And nothing was going to change much any time soon. I would be deluded to imagine I could be the one to break down these barriers. So I decided there and then that becoming a father was not for me. I would almost certainly have been as crap a dad as my dad. A convenient sperm donor whose only chance of seeing his puppies would be an accidental, guilt-ridden meeting on the common.

That was not for me. I was not going to be yet another feckless father. A puppy father on repeat. I would remain a single dog. True to my principles. I was going to choose my battles wisely. As Liz pointed out, it was hard enough changing perceptions of a dog's position in the workplace, without entering a whole new minefield. Keeping it simple. A day at a time.

Chapter 8

I seem to have got a bit ahead of myself on my voyage of self-discovery so let's rewind. It took about six months, but by the Christmas of 2015 I had just about got over the disappointment of no longer working in Westminster. Sure, the feelings of low self-worth got to me now and again – my dreams were often a horror show – but all things considered I was relatively content being a kept dog. I had pretty much resigned myself to not working in politics again. The Labour Party had changed and I hadn't. With Jeremy Corbyn now leader, there was a new breed of special adviser. Men and women in their twenties who looked even younger than Ed Miliband's bunch and who had spent the summer becoming fluent in dialectical materialism. It didn't feel like dogs were a high priority for the revolution.

There were still some habits I couldn't break. Like keeping up with the news every morning. But it was a relief not to be constantly worrying I had missed something important and would be found out when I got to work. Best of all was the knowledge that my days were pretty much my own once I had taken Jill or John for their walk. After that, I was mostly free to do what I wanted. Snooze, watch TV, meet friends. Snooze.

Canines Anonymous was a big help here. The meetings provided a sense of purpose, a structure, to my week. I had even taken up a commitment at the Tuesday meeting. My title was greeter and my job was to say hi to everyone, offer them a bowl of water as they arrived and to keep an eye open for any newcomers. Not the most onerous of tasks, but I hadn't been going to meetings that long myself. In truth and strictly between us, my favourite bit of the meeting was the after-party where we would all just go and hang out together near the cafe and talk nonsense to one another.

This was an ideal time for dog-watching. Here you got to see everyone at their most relaxed. Unguarded even. Take Danny. Danny's day job was as a guide dog, but his human let him out for a couple of hours on his own every week. You'd have thought that Danny was the most responsible dog you could ever meet. The eyes and ears of his human. And when he was working, he was all of that. The best in the business. But left to himself, he was hopelessly irresponsible. Wouldn't even wait for a green light to cross the road. A compulsive risk-taker.

Then there was Jerry. In meetings, he sounded like a spiritual giant. An old-timer who worked the steps religiously and always had something positive to say about how he used to find life difficult but now didn't. At first, I was hugely impressed by him. He had charisma. But listen to him talk after meetings and he wasn't so convincing, though the women dogs absolutely adored him. 'How are you feeling today, Jerry?' they would say. And Jerry would sigh, stare into the middle distance and say in a hushed whisper, 'A little bit of pain, a little bit of fear,' and be engulfed in cuddles for being the most sensitive dog in the fellowship. Only, I couldn't help wondering if it wasn't all an act as Jerry never looked like a dog in pain or fear. Maybe that was just the cynicism of Westminster I hadn't managed to cast off.

So all in all, I was as content. Things could have been a lot worse and I was just cruising towards Christmas, looking forward to turkey leftovers and stuffing. Possibly even the odd chipolata. Then everything changed when I received a phone call from a number whose identity had been withheld. I was tempted to ignore it as I had been getting a lot of calls from people trying to flog me health insurance. 'Make sure you're protected if you get ill and your humans haven't taken out cover for you,' they would say. Which did worry me as I happened to know that John and Jill had no insurance for me. 'It'll be fine,' they said. 'We'll just pay when necessary.' But would they?

Anyway, curiosity got the better of me, so I picked up. There was a brief silence and then a male voice.

'Is that Herbert Hound?'

'Er, yes. Who is speaking?'

'It's Ed Llewellyn, the prime minister's chief of staff.'

'What?'

'The prime minister would like to have a meeting with you . . .'

'Me?'

'Yes. Unlikely as it seems. And against my advice. But never mind. It's what the prime minister wants. Can you make the first week of January? Say Tuesday the fifth? First thing, at nine in the morning.'

'Um . . . Yes, I suppose so. That's great'

'Fine. Goodbye.'

Click.

I didn't even get a chance to say goodbye myself. I hadn't really been given time to think. Not even to ask why David Cameron wanted to see me. He didn't seem like the sort of man to arrange a meeting with a dog. Even me. But I guess Ed hadn't really seemed like a dog politician and that had worked out OK. Until it hadn't. My mind was racing. I just couldn't think what this was about. A dog who used to work for the Labour leader was being summoned to meet a Conservative prime minister. The best I could come up with was he was thinking of getting a dog for his family and wanted some advice on what breed might be best. Hmm. Still, at least I would get to have a look inside Number 10. Not many dogs got to do that.

I'm not sure why, but I didn't tell Jill and John about this call. It just seemed too surreal and I was worried they might think I was a fantasist. Best to tell them all about it afterwards. So, Christmas and New Year was a strange time. Part of me was fully engaged with my family and part of me was split off. Running through possible scenarios, trying not to let myself get ahead of the game. It was just a meeting. A meeting with the prime minister. Could mean anything or nothing.

On the morning of 5 January, I was up ridiculously early and, having warned Jill that her walk would be delayed to the afternoon, I headed off to Tooting Bec Tube. Westminster wasn't that crowded – most people seemed to be extending their holidays by an extra day – and I had time for a few nervous wees as I walked up Whitehall. At 8.50 am I presented myself at the Downing Street gates.

'No dogs here,' an armed policeman shouted.

'But I've got an appointment with the prime minister,' I replied.

'Of course you have. Now move along. As I said, no dogs.'

Finally, another policeman, waving a piece of paper, came to my rescue.

'Turns out this dog is to be admitted,' he said. 'Now run along through the security checks – make sure to take off your collar for the scanner – and don't make a mess anywhere.'

Charming. I'm a dog. Not an animal.

It felt special to be walking up Downing Street. This was history in the making. The first dog to be summoned to a meeting with the prime minister. This one was for dogs everywhere. I stopped briefly to pose for the cameras camped outside Number 10 and as I approached the building the door opened of its own accord. There to greet me was Larry the Cat.

'Piss off,' said Larry.

'Sorry?' I replied.

'This is my manor. Now, piss off.'

'I've got a meeting . . .'

'I don't care. There's only room for one quadruped round here. And that's me. I've outlasted loads of prime ministers and this is my patch. I get to say who comes and goes. I don't need any Herbie-come-latelys to mess things up. My house, my rules. Got it?'

This wasn't going at all to plan. I was anxious enough around cats as it was and the last thing I needed was a loud-mouthed, territorial cat. Thankfully, a nice woman called Camilla came to rescue me.

'You must be Herbert Hound,' she said.

How could she tell?

'Yes,' I replied.

'You are expected. Follow me.'

Larry gave me another filthy look as I was led towards the stairs. I tried not to catch his eye. No point in making unnecessary enemies. Up we went, past the photos of previous prime ministers, past rooms that appeared to be unused and then we came to a halt outside what I assumed must be David Cameron's office.

'Come in, Herbert,' he commanded.

'You can call me Herbie, prime minister. Everyone else does.'

'Great, then call me Dave.'

My first impression of Dave was that he was slightly taller than I had imagined. More substantial. His face glowed red. It was almost shiny. Reflective. Unlike him. Because most of all, he seemed entirely happy in his own skin. Someone who has never stopped to think how he had become one of the most prominent people in the country. He had been born to it. This was his birthright. At school and at university, he had been positively encouraged to believe that he was the Special One. Anywhere else, he would have been told to be more realistic in his ambitions. Most curious of all, he didn't even give the impression of working for it that hard. Being important came naturally to him.

'You're probably wondering why I've called you in here,' he continued. 'Well, let me get straight to the point. And I am going to have to trust you, so you won't let me down, will you?'

'Has a dog ever broken the trust of a British prime minister?'

'Good point well made. But here's the thing. You will remember that I promised my party a referendum on Britain's membership of the EU at the last general election . . .'

'Of course. You said the referendum would be held by the end of 2017.'

'Well, I've decided to go early. This summer. June to be precise.'

'How come?'

'Because I don't want it hanging over me for the next two years. The last thing I want is an ongoing war in the Tory party over Europe to drag on and on. An early referendum will lance the boil. Once we've won, the Eurosceptics will have to shut up. I don't want my legacy to be defined by an internecine war over our membership of the EU. I want it to be defined by . . .'

Dave's voice rather tailed off at this point and I decided not to push it. He was obviously having as much trouble thinking of what his legacy might be as I was. As far as I could see, his main political achievements so far were to completely stitch up the Lib Dems so they took all the flak for the coalition, to impose austerity on a country that was already struggling and to allow his health secretary to mess up the NHS with moronic reforms. Which didn't immediately make one optimistic for a glittering future. Still, maybe I was missing something. In any case, no point in rocking the boat on day one.

'I see, prime minister . . .'

'Dave.'

'Dave. And where exactly do I fit in? I'm not exactly plugged into the internal politics of the Tory party.'

'That's precisely the point, Herbie. I don't need you to keep an eye on the Conservatives. I've got plenty of people already doing that. What I need is someone who understands Labour. Can help get Labour supporters behind the campaign to stay in the EU. I just don't know any of the new Corbyn team and you have come highly recommended by a couple of my staff who have kept in contact with some of Ed Miliband's former advisers. They say you have a good political brain, good communication skills and can be trusted to be discreet.'

It was all very flattering. Me with a job in Downing Street. I'd thought I was out of the game and now I was right at the heart of government. OK, working with a Tory prime minister wouldn't have been my first choice but it wasn't as if Labour was likely to get into power any time soon. Christ, John and Jill went on and on about the Tories being in government for ten years. Just imagine if that was your entire life. So I was inclined to accept. Especially as it was a cause close to my heart. I had never met a dog who didn't believe in freedom of movement. Apart from a few elderly bulldogs. And they don't really count as they are against almost everything.

'You're not worried about a dog joining your team then, Dave?' I asked.

'Absolutely not,' he said. The same easy self-confidence that bordered on entitlement. Not a moment of doubt. I wished I could have had some of that. There's seldom a day goes past when I don't think I've screwed something up.

'Besides,' he continued. 'I feel like I've already had one dog on the team. During the coalition years,

Oliver Dowden was one of my special advisers and he was just like a not-very-bright puppy. Terribly keen, but basically useless. Which is why I made sure he was given a safe Conservative seat at the last election. Anything to get him out the way. There's no way you could be as hopeless as dear old Olive.'

'That's reassuring,' I said. 'So, what exactly is my job description?'

'Good question. It's Director of Purpose (Labour).'

'And what does that mean exactly?'

'Ah. It means that you are the director in charge of purpose of winning the referendum, with special responsibility for Labour. Your immediate line manager will be Craig Oliver who is Director of Purpose (Global) but you will also have occasional meetings with me to discuss how things are going. How does that sound?'

'I'm in,' I said.

'Good. And I'd like you to start tomorrow. Is that OK? You will be given a desk with the comms team on the ground floor.'

With a quick shake of the paw, I was dismissed. Dave returned to his desk and I let myself out of his office. At the bottom of the stairs, Larry was waiting for me.

'I suppose you think you're a big dog now,' he hissed.

News clearly travels fast in Downing Street. He must have been listening in on some of our conversation.

'Well, just remember who is boss around here,' Larry continued. 'No getting above yourself.'

'Absolutely,' I said. 'I'm just here to do my job. Not to take your place.'

Now was probably not a good moment to point out that my job was considerably more important than his. Catching mice is a very overrated skill. He should try chasing a squirrel. I left it at that. Though once the guard had let me out the front, I stopped to take a selfie. This was a moment to be cherished.

Jill and John weren't quite as pleased as I had hoped when I got home and told them the news. Yet again, they were worried that my job was taking me away from them and that I would find it difficult working for the Tories.

'Try to look at it this way,' I said. 'Imagine I'm a kind of civil servant. Obliged to work for whatever political party is in power. Besides, it's in a good cause. And you wouldn't like it if I was just lying around the house doing not very much except nagging you to come for walks.'

'You're right,' said Jill. 'We want you to be the best dog you can be. We don't want to be selfish and hold you back.'

They still looked a bit needy, so I walked over to the sofa and climbed up on their laps to give them a cuddle. They seemed to appreciate that.

The next day, I was up early and made it to Downing Street well before nine. No need for the security check this time: my pass was waiting for me at the gate.

Within seconds, I was shown in through the back entrance and taken to my desk. I was amazed. I had expected the office to be a hive of activity. Young men and women, fuelled by the self-importance of thinking they were running the country. Instead, it was completely empty but for me. I climbed up on my chair, logged on at my computer and tried out my new email address. Herbert.Hound@number10.gov.uk. My first message was to John. All it said was, 'It's me. Top of the world.'

It wasn't until about 10.30 that the rest of the Number 10 staff started to wander in. Even then they insisted on having at least one coffee before they settled down to do anything useful. Clearly, they operated on a different timetable to the rest of the country.

'What should I be doing?' I asked a woman sitting near me.

'I'm not sure,' she replied.

'Well, what are you doing?'

'I'm not sure.'

'By the way, I'm Herbie.'

'Great to meet you, Herbie. I'm Hannah. I suggest you just get on with what you've been told to do.'

'But I haven't been told to do anything. Other than be Head of Purpose (Labour) for the referendum campaign.'

The good news was that Hannah seemed in no way put out to be working alongside a dog. And neither did anyone else in Number 10. Apart from that little shit, Larry. It seemed that cynophobia might actually be a thing of the past in government. Perhaps Dave's 'Hug a Husky' message had finally got through.

The not-so-good news was that everyone just seemed intensely casual. Chillaxed to the max. It was as if Dave's sense of entitlement had become the predominant culture in the office. An effortless laziness. So much had been achieved with so little effort. Back in 2014, Cameron had comfortably won the Scottish independence referendum without trying too hard until the last ten days and he and his team clearly thought history would repeat itself with the EU referendum. They thought it was in the bag. Winning was what people like them did. The 2015 election merely proved their point.

Up on the wall was a chart mapping the latest opinion polls. It, too, suggested an easy win. By something like 65 per cent to 35 per cent. Far more comfortable than even the Scottish referendum. No wonder the Number 10 nerve centre was struggling to get excited. There appeared to be no jeopardy at all.

I glanced idly at my screen and decided I should at least do one thing. I drafted an email to both Seumas Milne and James Schneider, the two posh boys Jeremy Corbyn had drafted in to run the revolution. 'Hi,' I said. 'I'm now working at Number 10. Could we have a meeting to discuss Labour's co-operation in the Remain campaign?' Almost immediately, I got an out-of-office reply from both of them. 'I am away on annual leave. Unless it's urgent, please try again next week.'

Clearly the only one to think the referendum was a matter of some urgency was me. And maybe that was just my own confirmation bias. If I had a job, then it must be important. But what if I had the wrong end of the stick? Maybe the only reason I had been given the job was because it wasn't important. I was just some performative box-ticking exercise so that no one could later say that mistakes had been made in the operation. In which case, my main function was to be the fall dog.

This didn't really bear thinking about, so I tried to block it out of my mind. In any case, there didn't seem to be a lot more I could do that day. There was no point emailing Ed or any of the other Labour MPs whom I knew to be desperate to stay in the EU. They were all still in shock. First at having lost the election and then at the way Jezza had taken over the party. They were too terrified to say a word for fear of being purged.

The casualness became contagious. There are limits even to my work ethic. Having effectively done a full day's work within five minutes, I devoted the rest of the morning to getting to know the other members of the team and exploring the Downing Street garden. It was so nice to have a toilet nearby. And the food was to die for. Cumberland sausage and mash. One of my all-time favourites. Say what you like about Dave. He might have been one of the worst prime ministers in living memory, but he was probably the best boss I ever had.

That first week, there were a couple of surprises. One was the announcement that we would all be going off to a team bonding awayday the following week. All part of the touchy-feely management vibe that Dave wanted to instil in everyone in Number 10. Not that Dave would find the time to join us. No need, apparently. He was already a zen master. The complete human. At one with himself and the world around him. Almost everyone in the office groaned when they heard the news. Some had been on such exercises previously and knew what to expect. Others just couldn't see how it could possibly benefit them. I was rather looking forward to it. After all, it wasn't as if I had much else to do.

Then there was the Friday Email. This was a new one on me. At first, I thought I had just received my first personal email from Dave. Then I realised it had been sent to all staff. 'Hi,' said Dave. 'It has been another great week inside Number 10.' He then singled out four or five people to congratulate for their 'exceptional work' and signed off with the line that his plan for the country was working. It took Emily, who was part of the team working on the renegotiations with the EU, to decode what was actually going on here.

'It's the perfect passive-aggressive management style,' she said. 'Although the email says it comes from the PM it is actually written by Craig. Dave doesn't really have a clue what we're all doing. The purpose is to terrorise the staff and keep them on their toes. The fifty or so people who aren't mentioned in the email spend the entire weekend wondering why they weren't included and assuming that the boss class thinks they are rubbish. Meanwhile, those who do get a mention are often bewildered to find they are being praised for something they haven't done. So no one is ever happy. Everyone is a loser.'

The awayday was held at a management training centre just outside Henley. Even I struggled to see the point. We were all encouraged to be honest with one another and to say what we thought. But since when were a bunch of politically motivated men, women and dog ever honest with one another? Mostly, it was just everyone saying what they thought they were supposed to say. The 'break-out groups' were a particular waste of time. Especially the one on unconscious bias. Everyone pretending that they had never really noticed I was a dog. How many legs did you think I have? Still, for some reason we did all end up playing the Name Game. God knows why. If all else fails, I reckoned I might start running a few training courses myself. Along with giving inspirational talks. Shortly after I started work at Number 10, I got my first ever fan mail. A letter saying, 'I love you Herbie', from Grayson. Shame he was only four years old. But you've got to start somewhere.

Towards the end of January, I got an email from Ed. Llewellyn not Miliband. The prime minister would like a quick catch-up. His renegotiations with the EU were coming to an end and he wanted to get a feel for how much backing he could expect from Labour. Easier said than done. Despite repeated emails to James Schneider and Seumas Milne, I still hadn't been able to pin either of them down to a meeting. Just a one-line reply that they would get back to me soon. I got the feeling they weren't very interested in either me or the referendum.

So, I wasn't particularly looking forward to my meeting with Dave. I needn't have worried. As it turned out, he wasn't that interested in me either.

'How are you settling in, Herbie?' he began.

'Um. OK, I think . . .'

'Good, good. Pleased to hear it.'

I'm not sure what he thought he had heard because I hadn't really said anything.

'As you know,' Dave continued, 'I'm about to conclude a landmark new deal with the EU. It's going to be a game-changer.'

'That's terrific,' I said. 'Can you tell me some of the details?'

'Of course. But don't say a word to anyone else until we make the announcement. The long and short of it is this. The UK no longer has to be quite so enthusiastic about the EU. We will no longer be obliged to say we want ever-closer ties with the rest of Europe. Plus, we don't have to be so nice to EU migrants. We can delay paying them benefits. What do you think?'

I fell silent. Didn't quite know what to say. This was about the most feeble deal imaginable. Did he really imagine that it was going to change the minds of the

Eurosceptics? Hardly. If anything, it would encourage them to think they had been right all along. Then it dawned on me. The EU had given Dave next to nothing because it didn't see the point. It thought the UK would vote to remain, regardless. So, why make concessions? And Dave had gone along with this because he, too, thought the referendum was as good as won.

'Er . . . Are you sure it wouldn't be a better idea to delay the vote by a year? Give yourself more time to negotiate an improved deal. A chance to win over hearts and minds.'

'No,' he said. 'This is the right thing to do.'

Dave often used to say, 'This is the right thing to do.' As if he was following some divine purpose. I couldn't help wondering if this was his subconscious giving him away. Generally, it is only those who secretly think they might be doing the wrong thing who need to loudly insist they are doing the right thing.

'OK.' What else could I say? He wasn't about to change his mind.

'I'm sure most of the party will get behind me. Michael Gove has already given me his support.'

'Are you sure the Govester wasn't out of his head at the time? The one thing you can rely on is Mikey's disloyalty. He can't even be trusted with the petty cash in the office. Every time he pokes his head round the door, we have to move the dosh out of sight.'

'No. Michael is definitely onside. He gave me his word. Now, how do you think Labour will respond?'

'Your guess is as good as mine,' I said. What was the point in lying? 'They don't really appear to have engaged with the referendum as yet. They seem to be more interested in fighting among themselves and settling old scores with the right wing of the party at the moment.'

'I see. Well, keep at them.'

Was that it? Labour votes dependent on me alone. A cockapoo.

Just then, the phone on Dave's desk rang. He picked it up and listened. Just a few grunts in response before replacing the receiver.

'It seems that Gove has decided to back the Leave campaign,' he said. He appeared genuinely hurt. As if that had come as a huge surprise.

I took that as my cue to leave.

Chapter 9

We were where we were.

You'd have thought this latest bit of treachery by the Govester might have given Dave some pause for thought. A chance to delay the referendum until he had all his ducks in a row. No one would have cared. The only deadline was the one he had self-imposed. Not a bit of it. If anything, Gove had made him even more determined to stick to his schedule. As though it would be some kind of weakness for him to be deflected.

In any case, Dave's self-belief was unshakeable. Once he had made up his mind about something, it became a universal truth. The world and his will in full alignment. Doubt was for lesser mortals. He had chosen 23 June for the referendum because that was its preordained day. A day of triumph for him and the country. He was the new Britannia.

So what was a dog supposed to do except go along with it? Hell, he was probably right. That was his job, after all. The last thing he needed was a whole load of negativity from me. Time to give the worrying a rest and get on with my job.

A few days later, an email went out to all staff. The prime minister was going to announce the date of the referendum from outside Number 10 later that morning. This was a moment I was determined not to miss. A moment of political history. So I carefully jumped up on a chair from which I could look out of the window.

'Oi,' said Larry, when he showed up twenty minutes later. 'That's my spot.'

This time I wasn't backing down.

'I'm not moving,' I replied. 'But you can join me if you like.'

Grudgingly, he climbed up beside me. A temporary cessation of hostilities.

To be fair, Dave totally nailed the announcement. I mean, obviously a lot of it was total bollocks. Especially the bit about this being the chance to determine the questions the whole country had had about membership of the EU once and for all. Even a five-year-old could have told you the referendum was primarily a way of dealing with internal Tory party management. Those who still couldn't forgive the Germans for having started two world wars and those who thought they deserved a third chance. Or something like that. Most of the people I had met hadn't given the EU a second thought until the Tories started going on about it. Being able to live and work where you pleased and no trade barriers with your closest neighbours were easily a price worth paying for the occasional idiosyncrasy of the European parliament.

But what I really mean is that Dave was convincing at looking like and sounding like a prime minister. He had a sense of occasion. If not always the gravitas. I guess that's what comes of having been brought up to believe you are a member of the ruling class. You think you are serving the country when you are actually doing as you please. When Dave went along to his careers' adviser at Eton and said he wanted to become prime minister, no one batted an eyelid. He was merely told it might be useful were he to be given a safe seat first. No one needed to ask what party he might be standing for. Instead, he was given an introduction to the chairman of the Witney Conservative Association. At almost any other school, you'd have been kicked out of the careers office for taking the piss if you said you wanted to be prime minister. Or just told to go to the Job Centre like everyone else.

Dave, though, was delighted with the way the morning announcement had gone. So much so that he invited all Number 10 staff to an informal drinks party that evening. To give the team a boost ahead of the four-month campaign. My heart sank. Not that I was against hanging out with everyone, it was the standing up for hours I couldn't bear. No fun at all when you are at least five feet shorter than everyone else. Everyone ignores you or offers a half-arsed apology for standing on you.

Bang on the dot of 6.30, then, I rushed upstairs to make sure I was one of the first there so that I could bag one of the few chairs dotted around the side of the room and bunkered down. A member of the Downing Street catering staff reluctantly bought me a bowl of water. Sparkling, of course. I like to keep it classy. Then I just had to wait until people bothered to come over and talk to me. Only a few did and they didn't last long. Too busy scoping out more important people.

Dave finally showed up about three-quarters of an hour later and began by making an impromptu speech. How we were the finest team ever assembled in Downing Street – what did that say about the previous incumbents? – and that together we were going to make sure the UK remained in the EU. Because that was the right thing to do. And after we had won the referendum, we were going to get on with getting the country back on its feet. Because that was also the right thing to do. I did wonder if he realised he had just made many people a whole lot worse off with his six years of austerity. Perhaps that, too, was the right thing to do. But I kept that to myself. Largely because there was no one close enough to talk to.

Just as I was beginning to wonder if it might be time to skip off home – Jill and John needed a stroll on the common – I noticed Dave come towards me, flanked by his co-conspirator, George Osborne. They were clearly working the room. Giving everyone thirty seconds of their charm.

'How's it going, Herbie?' Dave asked.

I had learned by now it was best not to answer this question.

'You were terrific in front of the media today,' I said. And I sort of meant it.

'Can I get you a glass of wine?' he asked.

Dave was renowned for forcing alcohol on everyone. Classic enabler.

'No, thank you.'

'Are you sure? Not even a small one?'

'Are you trying to get me drunk? I had enough of that with one of your MPs, Mark Menzies. He got one doggy friend of mine totally pissed. That didn't end well. I'll stick to water.'

Dave changed the subject.

'This campaign is going to be rocky at times but the momentum is firmly with us. The Leavers only have Nigel Farage, whom most of the country can't stand, and a few oddball Tory MPs led by Gove. Just wait till Boris Johnson comes on board with me. Then we will be invincible.'

'Are you sure about Boris?'

'Absolutely. He's given me his word.'

'Mmm. He's given his word to an awful lot of women in his time. And been unfaithful to all of them.'

'That's a bit unfair, Herbie.'

'Not really. He's a professional treach. Genuinely. Given any opportunity to let someone down, he seldom resists. He just tells everyone what he thinks they want to hear and, once their back is turned, he does whatever he thinks is to his advantage. It's pathological with him.'

'Well, I trust him on this. We'll see what happens.'

We did see.

The day after, Boris wrote in the *Daily Telegraph* that he would be campaigning to leave – he'd also written a second article saying he would support Remain just in case he decided that suited his long-term career prospects better – the operations room in Number 10 was like a morgue. It seems that I had been the only one to see this coming. The dog wins again.

'I just can't believe he's done this,' Camilla said. She was close to tears. This was a betrayal she was taking personally.

'But it's Boris,' I said. He'd always been jealous that Dave had become prime minister before him. A battle of the Chosen Ones. He was even gutted that Dave had got a better degree than him. Even though neither showed few outward signs of intelligence. Eton and Oxford have a lot to answer for. So Boris had always been going to do the thing that caused Dave the most inconvenience. The thing that might one day get him into Downing Street.

Moments later, an email dropped from Dave himself. 'I know many of you will be shocked about the news. But now is the time to redouble our efforts. We are doing the right thing. The country is behind us. So, get back to work and let's make sure we get a large majority.'

Going back to work for the Director of Purpose (Labour) meant trying to pin down Seumas and James. Nearly two months into the job and I still hadn't even managed to arrange a meeting with them. Their interest in the referendum seemed minimal at best. Endless non-committal replies saying, 'Jeremy is very busy at the moment. Maybe next month,' didn't fill me with confidence. Busy doing what exactly? Giving another of his director's cut speeches on the Cuban revolution? The full three-and-a-half hours?

By now, I was getting slightly desperate. The rest of the office was consistently busy – or as Dave put it, 'working at pace' – but I was pretty much getting nowhere. I had tried bypassing the leader's office to see if I could get some members of the shadow cabinet interested in campaigning. Again, nothing. Nada. Just another blank. Not even John McDonnell, the shadow chancellor, could be bothered to answer. Clearly, what happened to the economy was beneath his pay grade. The only Labour MPs who seemed ready to stick their necks out were the likes of Kate Hoey and Gisela Stuart, who were campaigning for Leave.

I eventually tried Ed Miliband. Texting him to find out what the hell was going on in the Labour Party. He did at least reply. 'Can't really speak. There will be a show trial if I'm caught communicating with you. Careless talk costs lives. Don't use this number again.' I did wonder if I should press him further. Suggest going for a walk in St James's Park. But thought better of it. I still had a soft spot for Ed and didn't want to cause him trouble.

In April, there was a breakthrough of sorts. An email from Seumas. I was so surprised, I had to go outside for a wee. He was now ready to meet to discuss Jezza's involvement with the Remain campaign. Could I come over to his office in two days' time to go over the arrangements? It sounded like more of a command than a question. I checked my diary. Blank. As was every day. Fancy that.

Seumas was absolutely terrifying. And he didn't appear to much like dogs. He had an air of icy calm with a smile that never felt more than skin-deep. Someone who could be utterly charming to your face in the knowledge that he had ordered your arrest and execution only hours earlier. I wondered how well he slept at night. Whether his dreams gave him comfort. Probably. There's no justice in this world.

The leader's office was a complete tip. It hadn't been exactly tidy when Ed was in charge, but now it was a disaster. Papers everywhere, files left on the table and old pizza boxes tumbling out of the bins. Vegetarian, I assumed.

'Come in and sit down,' Seumas said, after James had opened the door for me. He made a small space on the table for me to put my notes. 'How can I help you?'

'I'd like to know your plans for the referendum campaign. Remain needs to have you on board.'

'Quite.'

'So . . . Ideally, we'd like Jeremy to come out on the campaign trail with the prime minister from time to time. To show that the government and the opposition speak as one on such an important issue.'

'That's not going to happen, I'm afraid.'

Here we go.

'Why not?'

'That's just not what Jeremy does. He can't be seen to share a platform with the Conservatives under any circumstances.'

'Not even for something as important as this?'

'Sorry.'

'Then what will Jeremy do?'

'He'll do one stand-alone speech. At the Senate House in London.'

Mmm. The model for George Orwell's Ministry of Truth. That should go down well. Not.

'And that's it?' I asked.

'That's it. That's all Jeremy has time for. He's very busy at the moment.'

I could see there was no room for manoeuvre. Best make the most of it.

'OK,' I said. 'But would you like some help with the speech? I can give you some lines that we've found particularly resonate with audiences.'

'Very kind. But no thanks. Jeremy writes his own speeches. He doesn't need the help of a Tory poodle.'

Rude. I'm only half poodle.

With that, the conversation – if you can call it that

– was over. The door miraculously swung open and I made my way back to Downing Street.

It was with a deepening sense of dread that I took the Tube to Senate House. This was meant to be my big gig. A rallying call for Labour voters. Set up by me. So, why did I think it was all about to unravel?

Seumas and Jezza arrived about twenty minutes before the event was about to start. By which time I was in a right state. Imagining the Labour leader might have had second thoughts. Seumas gave me a brief nod while Corbyn walked straight past me. He appeared to be in a world of his own.

He still was when he took to the podium and began speaking. The great communicator, the man who was meant to be able to sweet-talk people in their thousands with his passion, gave the impression he had accidentally overdosed on Valium. There was no affect in his speech, just a disconnected monotone. It was almost as if he wasn't really there and had sent a defective avatar instead.

'Labour is overwhelmingly for staying in,' he said. 'Labour is convinced it is better to reform the EU from within.'

But was he? This was more of a hostage video than a rallying cry for Remain. There was nothing on the benefits of the EU. No call to arms for the Labour activists. Just a grudging, 'We've had our differences but the EU has changed a bit since I voted against it in the 1975 referendum.' It felt like an exercise in existential alienation. If Dave was 'Project Fear' then Jezza was 'Project Apathy'. The EU was basically a bit rubbish, but being in it was a bit less rubbish than not being in it.

I rushed over to the woman in charge of the autocue. Anything to limit the damage. 'Tell him to show a bit more excitement. A bit more enthusiasm.'

That, too, backfired. Because it turned out that the only thing that raised a pulse in Jezza was attacking the Tories. It was David Cameron who had been responsible for blocking EU trade tariffs to prevent the Chinese from dumping steel. It was Cameron who had turned the UK into a tax avoidance industry. It was Cameron who was personally responsible for ensuring that 500,000 people would die from air pollution by 2025.

The Corbynistas in the audience started cheering at this point. This is what they had come for. Jezza now at least managed to open an eye. I would say he had found a second wind, only he had never found a first one. Corbyn went for the kill. 'It is Labour who would be behind the Forth Road package,' he said. No one had a clue what the Forth Road package was, but it sounded like a good thing. Stuff the EU, stuff dismantling the Brexit case, sticking it to the Conservatives was what really counted.

'Was that it?' asked several journalists in the Q&A that followed. 'That was all a bit . . . half-hearted.'

'I've never done anything half-hearted in my life,' Jezza said. Half-heartedly.

'Then why haven't you given any speeches on Europe before?'

'I've given lots of speeches.'

Just not on the EU. This was getting us nowhere and I longed for the event to end. Seumas and Corbyn hot-footed it out of the venue without even saying goodbye. I was beyond caring by now. I just wanted to meet up with a few pals on the common and forget about politics for a while. My tail didn't wag once for the rest of the day.

What on earth had possessed Ed Mil to allow hundreds of thousands of supporters to be given the right to vote for a leader for just £3? There were reports that loads of Tories had joined just to elect Jezza. Why had a few Labour MPs allowed themselves to think they were doing the right thing by nominating a token left-winger on to the ballot paper? With any other Labour Party leader, I'd have been living my best life. Touring the country, campaigning for Remain. Winning over hearts and minds. Making sure that dogs were free to live and work where they wanted. No paperwork, no painful vaccinations. It was just my luck to have to deal with a man who believed the EU was a globalist, capitalist conspiracy.

Still, at least Corbyn had made my life easier in one respect. I now knew there was no point pestering Seumas for any more public engagements. Quite the opposite. My job description had now changed to Director of Purposelessness (Labour). All my efforts were now spent on getting Jezza to do nothing at all. To stop Seumas even thinking of letting his boss making another appearance. He had already added hundreds of thousands of votes to the Leave campaign.

So now it was my turn to avoid Seumas. Occasionally he would email to suggest a meet to work out plans. Mostly I ignored them. Imagine being paid to not answer emails. To delete all messages as they came in. Mostly Seumas was as lacklustre as me, so he rarely followed up with a second email. But when he did, I would politely reply that the Grid was looking a little busy. Number 10 had plenty of people about campaigning for the next couple of weeks but I'd let him know if a day became available. In any case, we didn't want to overload Jeremy. We understood how busy he was and he'd done more than enough already.

Making sure Labour didn't do anything didn't take up more than about five minutes a day, so I gradually became more and more involved in the day-to-day running of the Remain operation. Primarily as an observer. Someone to keep an eye on what the Leave campaign was doing and to report back to the team.

It was actually a rather relaxing time for me. The weather was good and twice a week I would get on a train – free for dogs: amazing how many ticket inspectors assume you must be with a human – and just enjoy watching the countryside en route to some Leave event or another. Boris Johnson getting off the campaign bus in a market town to make a quick speech or Nigel Farage widening his crocodile smile while engulfed by his supporters.

The thing that most struck me was that they invariably seemed to be enjoying themselves. It was all a bit of a laugh to them and their supporters. Boris would just make it up as he went along. Telling lies was what he did best. He knew that the £315 million a week to the NHS slogan on the side of the bus was nonsense but he would just carry on repeating it. Largely because he knew that it wound up Remainers. He had even been instructed to stop using the slogan because it was misleading but that just encouraged him to double down.

Boris just enjoyed the attention. Any attention, good or bad. Just so long as he had an audience. And the crowds loved it. They knew that most of what he was saying was total nonsense. The EU is going to make it illegal to take fewer than thirty breaths a minute. The EU is going to ban the UK from calling the Channel the English Channel – but no one cared. Everyone was in on the joke. It was all a bit of a laugh. Who could be rudest about the EU. A modern-day Dad's Army, led by the Establishment men and women, sticking it to the Establishment Man. Just weird.

Farage was slightly different. Though he, too, was another Posh Boy narcissist who craved the limelight, he appeared to believe some of what he was saying. There was a nastier, more xenophobic edge to his speeches. Though he also seemed to operate in a closed thought system. Literally anything he didn't like was a result of Britain's membership of the EU. All we had to do to make the UK a global superpower was to leave the EU. The brilliance of this was that he never needed to prove anything because there was no proof required. If any industry was in trouble, it was down to Brussels. If you just happened to have woken up feeling a bit rubbish about your life, then that, too, was down to some EU diktat. Vote to leave and you'd be entering the land of hope and dreams.

Most of all, though, the Leavers seemed to be enjoying themselves. From stunts like sailing a flotilla of fishing boats up the Thames, which ended in a water fight with an angry Bob Geldof, to open-top bus rides, they had a monopoly on fun. Made it feel as if a vote to leave the EU was as much a lifestyle choice as a political one. Tick the right box and you would be embarking on an adventure. A holiday of a lifetime, where the sun always shines and you get to live out your dreams. Brexit could be anything you wanted it to be. You didn't even have to make up your mind whether to stay inside or out of the single market and customs union. You could change your mind from day to day, depending on whom you were talking to.

At one of the daily morning meetings in Number 10, I did try pointing this out. Maybe we could try and make the Remain campaign a bit more positive. Like pointing out all the good things that membership of the EU had done for us. The absence of war on mainland Europe. The freedom to go and live where you liked. Not that that really applied to me. I was quite happy in Tooting and would have been put out if John and Jill had said we were moving to Paris.

Nothing against the French but there aren't many parks inside the Périphérique. But you get my drift.

Instead, Dave and George seemed to spend their whole time saying how rubbish everything would be if we were to leave the EU. Things might not be ideal as they were, but they would be a whole lot worse if we left. Better the devil you know and all that. They somehow made the relationship with Europe feel toxic. Borderline abusive. One that we couldn't escape.

But no one wanted to listen to the dog. Least of all George. He had always had a problem with me. He needed to be the one in control. The one who was doing me a favour. He had a lot to learn. Ten days out from the referendum vote, the shit hit the fan with an opinion poll showing that Leave and Remain were neck and neck. Leave possibly even having a narrow lead. The operations team inside Number 10 went into a meltdown. Sheer panic. I chose to keep my head down. I had said my bit. If they hadn't listened to me previously, they weren't about to start now. In any case, it was probably all too late.

George had one last throw of the dice. He announced there would need to be an emergency budget if the UK left the EU. Huge tax rises and spending cuts to the health and education budgets. This could have been the death knell. We had long since entered a new world of post-truth politics. Nobody was trusted any more. People just believed the reality that suited them and almost no one thought that George was telling the truth. I'm not even sure if George knew whether he was bluffing or not.

I spent most of the day of the referendum at home. Going for walks with the humans and watching *Lassie* on the TV. But it was impossible to relax as I had this overwhelming sense of despair. It had been ours to win and we had blown it. Now I just wanted the whole thing over and done with. It had been a long campaign and I was feeling knackered.

Round about eight in the evening, I headed off to Westminster to watch the results come in with the team at Number 10. Most people started the night feeling positive. We must have done enough, surely? But come about 2 am when the result came in from Sunderland, despair began to set in. By around 5 am, it was clear the game was up. Some people were crying. I chose to go out for a walk in the near-deserted streets to clear my head. Just outside the Commons I bumped into the Tory Brexiteer David Davis, who had been up all night giving TV interviews to anyone who would listen.

'Good morning, Herbie,' he said.

'If you say so. I guess it's over to you now.'

'Don't you worry about a thing. The transition will be seamless. Everyone will be queueing up to do trade deals with us.'

'Hmm.'

I left David to his jollity – it didn't feel right to spoil his excitement quite so soon. And besides, maybe he was right. So, I returned to Downing Street where things had got even more chaotic. Larry the Cat was loving it. He'd never much cared for Dave and was taking bets on when he would resign. Not that there was any sign of Dave. He had apparently locked himself upstairs in his flat with Sam and was refusing to come out. Brilliant. The country had only gone and delivered one of the biggest shocks to the political system in a generation and its prime minister had nothing to say about how it would work and what would happen next. A total failure of leadership. In the meantime, the financial markets had opened, knocking £100 billion off the stock market in a matter of hours.

It wasn't until after 9 am that the lectern was finally brought out into the street. I raced outside to get a top spot outside Number 11. This was a speech I wasn't going to miss. Half an hour later, Dave and Sam came out together. So, this was to be a resignation affair. Who would have guessed? Only a few days previously, Dave had insisted he would stay on if the country were to vote Leave. To see us through the upheaval. 'The Right Thing to Do'. That aged well. Apparently, the right thing to do is sometimes the wrong thing to do.

Dave mumbled a few words. The country had made its decision. He made no effort to conceal the fact he thought it was the wrong one. Britain's economy is still fundamentally strong, he insisted. Mmm. He obviously hadn't been following the FTSE 100. 'I love this country, and I feel honoured to have served it,' he said, his voice beginning to crack. 'And I will do everything I can in future to help this great country succeed. Thank you very much.'

Though he wouldn't be doing anything much in the meantime because he would be quitting as prime minister within a matter of months. There were obviously limits to his sense of public service. Dave and Sam considered a kiss for the cameras but decided against. Instead, he started humming to himself as he headed back indoors. Outside on Whitehall you could hear someone playing 'Land of Hope and Glory'. It was that kind of day.

There were plenty more tears back in the operation room. A chorus of 'Such a great speech.' 'So dignified.'

'Er . . . Excuse me,' I said. 'But Dave got us into this mess through his own carelessness. A referendum promise to win him a general election. He could have delayed it. He could have rigged it by demanding Leave reach a super majority of 60 per cent. But no, he thought he knew best. Now he's left the country in a mess and has just wandered off. I'm not sure I call that a public service. He will be just fine. Big bucks on the speaking circuit. £800K for his memoirs. It's the rest of the country that will be screwed.'

I fell silent. I could sense this was the wrong speech at the wrong time. Dave's faithful retainers weren't in the mood for this from a dog. I had said too much. I retreated to my desk to watch the Vote Leave winning acceptance speeches. Surely they would give us a clue about what would happen next? Wrong again.

Boris and the Govester turned up forty-five minutes late for their gig and when they did show their faces they looked just as shell-shocked as Dave. If I didn't know better, I'd have guessed they had been up all night on a drink and drugs rampage and had just come down to find they had inadvertently murdered their best friend. Both could hardly utter a coherent sentence. Nor had they any sense of responsibility for what they had done. They had never intended to win the referendum. Just to come a close second and enhance their political careers.

I switched off my computer. As ever, there had been radio silence from Labour. Jezza was probably too busy giving celebratory high-fives to everyone in Labour HQ. No matter, my job was done. All the grown-ups had long since left the room. When a dog can tell this was no way to run a country, then you know the game is up. It was time to go home.

Chapter 10

It was about this time that things became weird.

With the government in limbo, the rest of the country seemed to be falling apart in a collective existential crisis. Brexit seemed to have tipped everyone over the edge. Those who had voted Remain were in a tailspin. Threatening to leave the country or trying every trick in the book to acquire Irish or Portuguese passports. This was the end of days, they sobbed. The UK as they knew it was finished. Meanwhile the Leavers declared war on all experts – anyone can be a surgeon these days – and took every opportunity to drape themselves in the flag of St George and shout that this was the greatest day in the country's history since the German surrender in 1945. Though their elation was tempered with fury that Remainers were being unpatriotic by not joining in their ongoing celebrations.

This alienation and tribalism even filtered down to meetings of Canines Anonymous. Not just dogs sharing about their humans' erratic behaviour, though there was a lot of that. But mutts actively joining in the hysteria. Staffies and bulldogs dressing up in Union Jack collars and bandanas. Picking fights with schnauzers and Alsatians. Barking at them to go home. Then there were the rottweilers launching their own counter offensive. Humming Beethoven's 'Ode to Joy' while English sheepdogs were sharing their experience, strength and hope. I know CA is meant to be a safe space but it can sometimes be a hotbed of resentments. I just tried to keep a low profile.

Westminster was little better. Every politician did their best to be grown-up in public. What's done was done. The people had spoken. This always confused me. The referendum had been won with 52 per cent of the vote, which meant that nearly half the country had thought Brexit was a bad idea. But the 48 per cent were about to be written out of history.

Behind closed doors, though, MPs and special advisers were no better than the rest of the population. Teeming with grudges that would be settled over the coming years. They would even be coming for me. But I was determined to hang around in Number 10 for as long as possible. Just to soak up all the madness. To be at the centre of things as events unravelled during the last few months of Dave's time in office.

It didn't quite work out like this. Because into a political vacuum stepped a human vacuum in the shape of Theresa May. Almost no one saw that one coming, as it had been widely assumed that Boris would be the next incumbent of Number 10. He was the one responsible for Brexit, so he was the one with the popularity to deliver it. Only Boris never put himself forward for the leadership of the Tory party. On the morning he was due to make the announcement, the Govester declared that he had never thought Boris was fit to run the country; what took him so long? He had only been campaigning with him for the past four months, so he could have let us know sooner – and would be putting himself forward as leader. The drugs that man must have been on.

Of course, there was nothing stopping Boris from still running. He'd almost certainly have won anyway. But Boris can't handle any challenge. He crumples. Typical of a man with a big ego and no self-worth. So, he bottled it. Which left just five people hoping to be prime minister. The Govester, Stephen Crabb, Liam Fox, Andrea Leadsom and Theresa. Crabb and Fox were knocked out early. Crabb because no one knew who he was and Fox because everyone knew who he was. Then Mikey because he couldn't be trusted not to stab himself in the back.

So that left just Andrea and Theresa, who were then meant to tour the country going head to head in hustings before the Tory membership got to have the final say. Only, within days, Andrea had dropped out. Partly because she was completely useless – imagine if she had ended up running the country – but mainly because she had been caught out twice saying that Theresa would be unsuitable because she didn't have any children. Which left Theresa as the last person standing. She had become prime minister without ever having said a word. She says it best when she says nothing at all.

Dave was furious. As were the rest of the Downing Street team. We had all imagined we had until October to swan around doing nothing very much. Dave had been desperate to do one last world-leaders' shindig at the G20. To get a few autographs presumably. Now, though, he and all of us would be kicked out by the middle of July.

Come the changeover day, I was as usual one of the first in. I again wanted to make sure I had one of the best places in the street to hear the speeches. Dave's was classic Dave. All about how he alone had made the country and the world a safer, stronger place. I exchanged glances with Camilla. How could he say all this with a straight face? I mean, if everything was so fantastic, how come he had been forced to resign?

About an hour later, Theresa returned from the Palace and gave her own speech. She wanted to be nice to black people. That was a start, I suppose. She wanted everyone to partake in society. She wasn't going to govern for the privileged few. I quickly texted Ed Miliband. She appeared to have ripped off one of his speeches. This was what he had been promising the country a year ago. At about the same time as Theresa, in her capacity as home secretary, had been sending around vans with 'Go Home Foreigners' on the side.

Once the photographers had got the picture of Theresa entering Number 10, we all trooped back inside. Most of the operations team had packed up their desks in advance. They knew what was coming. I, though, had a plan. I wanted to see if I could hang around for a while longer. I had got used to the excitement of working in Number 10. So, when Nick Timothy and Fiona Hill, Theresa's right-hand man and woman, came into the room, I curled up out of sight under the desk.

'What are you doing?' asked my soon-to-be-ex-colleague Beth.

'Sssh,' I replied, putting my paw over my mouth.

Nick clapped his hands.

'OK, everyone,' he said. 'You know how this works. You've got ten minutes to take yourself and your personal items out of the building. The new team will be arriving in half an hour.'

I must have dozed off. It was very cosy under the desk. The next thing I knew a whole lot of strangers were entering the room. I climbed up on my chair, trying to make it look as if I had just got here, too. And it worked a treat. Everyone had forgotten about the dog. They always do. Even Nick and Fiona. They must have both thought that the other one had reappointed me. Either way, no one asked me what I was doing there again. I was now part of the furniture. Just one more thing to do and my transition would be complete. Take down the sign that said 'Director of Purpose (Labour)' from on my desk. That was too obviously a David Cameron kind of job. Replace it with 'Executive Officer Brexit Delivery (Labour)'. Much better. I now looked like Team Theresa.

One other thing had changed. Larry seemed to have ceased hostilities with me. More than that, he started to go out of his way to be friendly. I'm not sure quite why. Maybe he was just tired of being angry the whole time. Or maybe he had realised I was no real threat and had decided he quite liked having another quadruped about the place. Now he made a point of giving me a cheery wave each morning when I arrived and I would share a tuna sandwich with him over lunch.

Once I was reasonably settled back in the office, Larry came to seek me out. 'Psst,' he said. 'Follow me.' I jumped off my chair and did as I was told. First stop was the Downing Street front door. Here he extended his claws and started scratching a mark in the door frame.

'What are you doing?' I asked.

'Keeping a tally,' he said. 'I've now seen off one prime minister. Let's see how many more I can outlast.'

We both sniggered. Then Larry took me upstairs and told me to wait outside Theresa's study. 'She's about to start appointing her cabinet,' he said. 'This is always a real laugh. If you put your ear to the door you get to hear MPs pleading for their careers or overwhelmed with sycophancy as they get a promotion. It's totally unmissable.'

First on the agenda was a phone call to George

Osborne. He was getting the sack. This was done on speakerphone and George was not happy. Not surprising really. Imagine being replaced by Philip Hammond. George had always rather dismissed Theresa when he and Dave were running the show. Had taken the piss out of her social awkwardness. She wasn't quite as posh as either of them. So, you could hear the pleasure in Theresa's voice as she told him the good news. George hung up in a huff, having told her she would regret it. Though it didn't sound as if she would. Larry and I high-fived one another.

Next up was the Govester. He arrived in person, clearly hoping for a promotion.

'May I congratulate you on your stunning victory in the leadership contest,' he began. 'I have always said that you are just the prime minister the country needs to get us through these tumultuous times.'

He didn't seem to realise it was partly down to him that things were falling apart.

'Shut up, Gove.'

He paid no attention and carried on talking.

'It will be an honour to serve you. Now, how best can I be of use to you? Perhaps as home secretary . . .?'

'Shut up and listen. I've come to the conclusion that your natural instincts for treachery and disloyalty are best rewarded with a return to the backbenches. You're sacked.'

'B-b-but what shall I tell my wife? She will be furious with me if I don't have a ministerial post. Have you not got anything for me? It doesn't have to be in the cabinet. I'll do anything.'

'You're sacked.'

'Y-y-yes, Theresa. I mean prime minister. Whatever you say.'

'You can go now.'

Poor Mickey was almost in tears as he left her study. Larry and I were rolling on our backs killing ourselves with laughter, so he had to step over us. This might just have been the best ten minutes of our entire lives.

Then the big one. Boris. He looked utterly bewildered to have been summoned. As were Larry and I. He didn't have a cabinet post to be sacked from.

'Don't sit down,' snapped Theresa. 'This won't take long. I'll get straight to the point. You know full well that I can't stand you.'

'Mmm.'

'Good. We understand each other perfectly. Which is why I propose to make you foreign secretary. Better to have you inside the tent pissing out. Rather than outside pissing in, I want you to be out of the country for as much of the time as possible. Having you embarrass yourself on the world stage will be a sign to our trading partners that we are open for business.'

Boris never could resist a bit of abject flattery.

'Thank you, prime minister. It will be an honour to meet black people with watermelon smiles and women in burkas who look like letterboxes.'

'That's exactly the kind of casual racism I'll be looking for from you. Putting the Great back in Great Britain. You can go now.'

The rest of the afternoon was almost as much fun. Andrea Leadsom furious to be told she would become environment secretary. She was hoping for something much better. But Theresa told her it was the ideal post for a mother. Then Chris 'Failing' Grayling. The politician who had never found a job that he couldn't do badly. He was off to become transport secretary.

'But I was your campaign manager for the leadership,' he whined.

A contest Theresa had won precisely because Failing had had to do nothing.

'That's why you're getting transport. Count yourself lucky.'

That was about it for the day. I gave Larry a hug.

'I owe you one for this,' I said.

'Think nothing of it,' he replied.

That was just about it for the summer. Recess couldn't come too soon. Everyone in Westminster was completely knackered, me included. It had been a tough year so far and I needed a break. I also needed to spend a bit of time with John and Jill to reconnect with them. Fair to say, they were getting worried about me.

'Are you sure you really want to be doing this?' asked Jill, as we all went for a walk together in Richmond Park.

'How do you mean?' I replied.

'Well, you've been working in Westminster for the best part of two years now. That's fourteen of your years. Give or take. Do you think you might need a break?'

Then John piled in.

'It's also getting embarrassing. It was fine when you were working for Ed Miliband. That was something we could all get behind. It was just about OK when you were working for Cameron because at least you were the Labour point dog in the Remain campaign. But now you are working for a Tory prime minister trying to deliver a Brexit policy with which you don't agree. Whatever happened to your promise to live your values? One of the things we always loved about you was your sense of right and wrong. For ages you were our moral compass. Now look at you.'

I trotted off for a piss. Momentarily distracted by the scent of a deer. Delaying tactics. I didn't quite know what to say. Because there was some truth in what they were both saying. And it had been on my mind as well. Was I really selling my soul just to get close to the centre of power? Was I no better than all those SpAds and researchers I used to look down on for their naked ambition? Had I become the thing I always used to despise?

'You're right to be concerned,' I said on my return, after losing track of the deer. 'I have become a bit of a dick. I promise to try to do better. But I do genuinely love what I do. It's not often a dog lands himself in such a fascinating job. I feel it's my role not to give up.

To be an inspiration to others. That there's more to life than just going for a walk, wolfing down your dinner and having an afternoon snooze on the bed. More even than herding sheep or guiding blind people. Important though those jobs are.

'Do I get a kick out of what I do? Yes. I can't deny I like it when I get recognised. I must be one of the most photographed dogs in Britain. Papped every time I go in and out of Downing Street. But I have got my paws firmly on the ground. I haven't tried to monetise my fame by creating my own Instagram account. And I do believe I can be a force for good. It's not as if I've become a Tory. I'm still a Labour dog at heart. And my new role is to keep Labour in the loop. Besides, someone's got to try and get the best Brexit deal for the country. There's no point on relying on the government.'

I was very naive back then. Those words would come back to haunt me.

But I seemed to have reassured John and Jill a little bit. At any rate, they never put any more pressure on me to stop what I was doing. All they wanted was the best for me and I appreciated that. Time for a group cuddle and a pub lunch.

The rest of the summer passed all too quickly. John and Jill went off to Spain to stay with some friends for ten days. I chose to stay at home. I'm not good in the heat, so I went off to look after some other humans, Kim and Sarah, who were in need of some company. Other than that, I just mooched around. Did some reading – I was in my Anthony Trollope phase at that point – and even went to Glyndebourne to see *The Marriage of Figaro*. The final redemption scene gets me every time.

Back at work in September and there was a strange vibe in Downing Street. A peculiar hybrid of complacency and intense anxiety. It didn't take a genius to realise why. The opinion polls had the Tories miles ahead of Labour, so no one wanted to do anything to rock the boat. Yet everyone knew that something had to give. Sooner or later, someone was going to have to do something about Brexit. To stop just saying everything was going to be great and get round to defining what Brexit meant. And everyone in the operations room where I was working had clearly decided that Brexit was well above their pay grade. No one wanted to be the one to suggest something that would almost certainly go wrong or be criticised for being the wrong kind of Brexit. So, everyone worked very hard at doing nothing. The more hours they spent in the office, the less they did. Even Nick and Fiona. The louder they shouted at everyone, the less effectual they were.

What everyone was waiting for was a sign from Theresa. A puff of white smoke to indicate that she had made a decision. Or something approaching a decision. A decision that she wasn't able to make a decision yet would have been a start. But she remained resolutely gnomic. From time to time, she would be forced into saying 'Brexit means Brexit' during a prime ministerial statement in the Commons. Tory MPs would publicly declare this to be a model of clarity while in private saying they, too, were in the dark. Clueless even.

Theresa was a total mystery to me. In fact, I often wondered if she was a mystery to herself as well. Or maybe she had just created this impenetrable carapace in order to survive as a successful woman in the Tory party. Anything to keep other people at arms' length. She had this way of looking through you as if you were invisible. Conversation with her was painful. Her speaking voice was almost inhuman. A disconnected monotone. And you could never tell if she was listening. She could reduce some people to tears with her silences. Cabinet ministers would often complain to us that they had thought they had secured her agreement, only for her to do the opposite.

No one had really known what she had thought about leaving the EU in the run-up to the referendum. She had mumbled something about being in favour of Remain at the start of the campaign to keep her Maidenhead constituency on board, but then had become an elective mute. Saying nothing whatsoever. As if she didn't really care that much one way or the other. Just wanted to make sure she had done her utmost to remain on the fence so she could align herself with whichever side won at the end. It was the story of Theresa's life. The shadowy, charmless presence who played the political percentages and ended up making friends with no one. You'd be hard pushed to find anyone in the Tory party who really liked her. Who held her in affection.

The longer Theresa stuck to 'Brexit means Brexit' the more feverish the speculation became. Leavers because they wanted a sign that Number 10 had got to grips with the issue and Remainers because they concluded the government still didn't know what it was doing. They were right. I was there and I can promise you everyone in Downing Street was equally confused. To add to the sense of the surreal, the government was busy saying it wanted the prerogative to trigger Article 50, the UK's formal notice that we would be leaving the EU, without an act of parliament. This ended up with the government losing in the Supreme Court, which only added to the sense of chaos. It was beyond me. The *Daily Mail* calling the judges 'Enemies of the People', while Theresa wanted to give notice to leave without knowing what kind of Brexit she wanted. Go figure.

While most of my colleagues spent their days googling 'Brexit means Brexit', hoping for some divine AI intervention, I was surprisingly busy. You'll remember that during my time working for Dave as the Labour liaison dog I was consistently given the brush-off by Seumas and James, who couldn't have been less interested me. Well, now they bombarded me with emails – one or two a day – saying how good it would be to meet up and, by the way, what was the government thinking on Brexit? By and large, I just deleted these emails after reading them. Didn't bother to respond. I mean, what could I possibly say? I knew about as much as they did.

But, eventually, they made me an offer I couldn't refuse. How about I joined them and Jeremy in Jezza's favourite Cuban restaurant in Waterloo? I couldn't say no. I absolutely love Cuban food. Now, I know it's not to everyone's tasted but rice, beans and chicken are my meal of choice. I'd eat that every day if I could.

'How are you getting on at Number 10?' asked Seumas.

'Fine,' I said. Keeping it non-committal. And there was an element of truth to it. A general sense of chaos and cluelessness was just fine, as far as I was concerned.

'Jeremy would like to know what the Brexit plan is. Wouldn't you, Jeremy?'

'The treatment of the Palestinian people is an outrage,' said Jezza.

'We're here to talk Brexit,' said James. Trying to keep his boss on message.

'The only good Brexit is one that recognises an independent state of Palestine,' Corbyn continued.

'I'm not sure that's top of the government's Brexit agenda,' I said. 'But I will be sure to pass on your thoughts back to Number 10.' Like hell I would.

But all in all, it was turning into a better lunch than expected. Jezza didn't really want to talk about Brexit and I certainly didn't. So, instead, he went into long rants about marches he had been on and picket lines he had manned. To round things off, James didn't really like what he had ordered, so I got to eat his as well as mine. A two-lunch day is always a good day.

Come January 2017, Theresa had more or less made up her mind. Or, more likely, had had her mind up for her. Like Dave, she was terrified by the Eurosceptic lunatics on the right of the party. As someone who had once, possibly, whispered Remain, she was desperate not to look as if she was too soft on the EU. So, at a speech at Lancaster House, she announced what Brexit would look like. Or the rough outlines, at any rate. She was very conscious, she said, that the referendum vote had been tight, so she wanted a Brexit that would be acceptable to both Leave and Remain. But at the same time, she was at pains to point out that the referendum had been won overwhelmingly by Leave and so she was going to go for the hardest possible Brexit. That meant leaving the single market and the customs union. Apparently, this meant that Global Britain was open for business. Yeah, right. Trash your European neighbours with whom you did 40 per cent of your trade. Watching this on the TV back in Number 10, I did wonder if she was unwell. Or whether she had been taken hostage by forces unknown. Judging by the murmurs coming from some of the European ambassadors in the audience, they were thinking much the same.

I suppose that at least we had some clarity. Once back in Number 10, Nick and Fiona were punching the air. That was the Brexit the country had voted for, they shouted. And all the Number 10 team, who had literally spent the last six months doing nothing, joined in. All their enforced idleness had paid off.

But before Theresa got Tim Barrow, the UK's representative to the EU, to hand over the UK's withdrawal notice – it's not you, it's me – there was an EU council meeting for Theresa to attend. This was my big chance, because none of the other special advisers wanted to go. They worried their careers might be affected if they were seen to be too nice to the EU. But I wasn't particularly bothered. I figured that if anyone had wanted to fire me, they would have done so by now. Besides, it turned out that people quite liked having a dog around. Many even used to confide in me. Man's best friend and all that. Their stories are safe with me. I don't do kiss and tell.

What swung it for me was that I was also one of the only advisers who would admit to speaking French. My poodle upbringing. Back in Number 10, there was a culture of fear. Anyone who spoke a European language was in danger of being labelled a traitor. But somehow a dog being fluent in French was no big deal. How quickly people forget that George Orwell was half-French. I'm surprised his books haven't been banned.

So early one Monday morning, I turned up to Stansted airport to fly to Brussels with the prime minister. I had been dreading the journey. An hour making small talk with Theresa. I shouldn't have worried. She didn't say a word. Not even 'Good Morning'. Instead, she just opened her red box and started reading her briefing notes. Which meant I could enjoy the leather seats and stare out the window.

On arrival in Brussels, Theresa had a meltdown when she found she had been scheduled to give her speech in the graveyard 1 am slot.

'Ask that man why I am number fifteen on the order paper,' she insisted.

I did as I was told.

'*Parce-qu'il n'ya pas un numero seize*,' he laughed.

'What did he say?' Theresa asked.

'He said something of this importance deserved a special slot. One where no one would be rushed. He also assured me it was the best-attended time of the meeting. No one would want to miss a word.'

Come 1 am and it was just Theresa and a dozing minister from Slovenia in the room.

Where was everyone, Theresa wanted to know. I wandered off to find a spokesperson for the EU president.

'*Parlez a la main*,' she said.

Umm. Everyone was watching via a live feed in their hotel rooms, I told her. It was too important a speech to be heard in person. It didn't seem the moment to tell her that the EU wasn't in the mood to do the UK any favours.

But it turned out that Theresa had other things on her mind. Having repeatedly told the media that she didn't need a personal mandate and wouldn't be calling a general election, she had decided over the Easter recess that she did need a personal mandate and would be calling a general election. Something about the twenty-point lead she had over Labour in the polls had helped her to reach this conclusion. Time to show the country she was more able than she looked.

And that was effectively that for me. For the time being, at least. Nick and Fiona made it clear they didn't want me anywhere near the team writing the manifesto and, with the government more or less coming to a halt for the campaign, I was rather left to my own devices. No one cared that much if I came or went, so I spent most of the time either at home or going for a walk by myself in St James's Park.

More fool Nick and Fi. I was no fan of Theresa – it was unnerving the way she could suck any energy out of a room like a black hole – but if I had been asked, I would have told them it didn't sound like a good idea to tell one of your core demographics that you would effectively have to bankrupt yourself if you needed care for dementia. But Nick and Fi had been dead set on the idea. Grab the bull by the horns and deal with a problem all governments had tried to avoid. No better time to do it when the polls are indicating you will get a one-hundred-seat majority.

But no one had counted on Theresa's uncanny ability to self-destruct. The manifesto launch was a total disaster. She hadn't even bothered to tell her cabinet what was in the manifesto and they all looked shell-shocked when they discovered what they would be asked to sell to the country. Within days, the whole thing unravelled as Theresa announced at another event that 'nothing had changed', when everything had changed. The dementia tax was summarily dropped.

After that, Theresa rather fell apart for the rest of the campaign. Resorting to shouting 'strong and stable', when she looked as if she was having a breakdown. Corbyn, meanwhile, was having the time of his life. Having been barely monosyllabic during the referendum, you now couldn't get him to shut up. If he had showed half this passion the previous year, we wouldn't have been in this mess. Everywhere he went, his supporters greeted him like the Messiah. It was all very odd.

My biggest excitement was that ITV had invited me to be part of their election-night coverage. 'We've never had a dog on before,' said the booker. Slightly unnecessarily. 'But we think you'll be a brilliant addition to our team.' It was all very flattering and on the Thursday afternoon of election day I went to have a haircut. I wanted to look my best.

What a night that was. Starting with the exit poll. Although Theresa's lead had narrowed slightly in the last week there wasn't any pundit in the country who didn't think that a Tory government with an increased majority was a foregone conclusion. At 10 pm, we learned that no overall majority with the Tories the largest party was the most likely outcome. Across the studio, I could see George Osborne laughing hysterically. He really did hate Theresa. He could certainly bear a grudge.

The rest of the evening was a rollercoaster. Various Tories in a state of shock. Every Labour supporter acting as if they had won. Not losing by as much as you expected was the new winning. As I said at the start, this was all getting weird. But I loved it. Any nerves I had about being on TV soon passed. All you had to do was talk in the same clichés as everyone else.

'It's still very early in the count.'

'Sunderland will be a good guide.'

'The exit poll is usually accurate.'

'We're seeing the same swing across the country.'

That sort of thing. Honestly, you could do it, too. It's surprisingly easy.

I left the studio at about four in the morning. Having nothing better to do, I wandered back to Downing Street. There were about three or four other people in the office. They all looked devastated, so I kept my feelings to myself and went to find Larry. He was busy eyeing up the doorpost.

'I think it's a bit early for that,' I said.

'It's only a matter of time,' he replied.

A couple of hours later, Theresa returned from her constituency. She rushed upstairs without saying a word to anyone. From outside her office, I could hear loud, heaving sobs.

Things had just got even more interesting.

Chapter 11

It has just occurred to me that I might have been doing this all wrong.

Having recently reread an assortment of political memoirs and biographies, I couldn't help but notice that the majority are entirely self-serving. Careers on an endless upward trajectory, only stalled by the incompetence of others. Every decision taken was the right one, often accompanied by pages of self-justification. Every small triumph elevated to one of national importance. Even when they were wrong, they were right. Their only failing to have been surrounded by politicians less able than themselves. Let down by a country that lacked the intelligence to appreciate the brilliance of their betters. Whatever happened to a bit of gratitude?

Only that's not quite the way this book is shaping up. Because by any objective standard my career to date has been an abject failure. There's no escaping it.

Not even David Cameron, who three years after he left office in disgrace managed to recast his career as one of heroic public service. He had the cheek to call his book *For the Record*, when it would be better filed under fiction. Even Dave would have been stumped by my achievements so far.

To recap. I was hired by Ed Miliband to improve his public image. Well, that went well. OK, so I was cut out of the loop by Dan but who will remember that? And maybe no one could have sold Ed to the country back in 2015. He's a lot more confident now than he was then. But the net result was that I failed. Labour did worse than expected in the general election and Ed resigned. Played one, lost one.

Then I was hired by Dave to work on the Remain campaign in the referendum. Should have been a walk in the park, given the opinion polls three months before the vote. I had one job. To get Jeremy Corbyn to campaign hard enough to get Labour voters out in force behind staying in the EU. OK, again there were mitigating circumstances. Dave was fairly rubbish himself at selling Remain and nobody has ever made Jezza do anything he didn't want to. In his own way, he has the same feelings of entitlement as many prominent Tories. It's his way or no way. But either way, the net result was that Remain lost. Played two, lost two.

Which brings us up to the present. Arguably, here I have the least personal culpability. I was never a key player in the first year of Theresa May's government. Neither Nick nor Fiona could ever work out which one had hired me – neither had – and so I rather invented my own job description. But the bottom line didn't lie. I was part of the Number 10 team that was both supposed to be delivering Brexit and ensuring the government functioned properly. A tough job, maybe, given the raw materials. Selling someone as odd as Theresa to the country was always going to be an uphill struggle. But we failed. The general election had been a catastrophe for her. So, played three, lost three.

Not great, is it? Now, you could say that it doesn't really matter what I achieved. The important thing was that I was there at all. The first dog ever to have become a special adviser, not just for Labour but also for the Tories. To have worked at the centre of government. Only I don't want people to make allowances for me. To be remembered as the token dog who smashed the glass ceiling when most of his mates just wanted to chase squirrels on Tooting Bec Common. I want to be judged as an equal.

So now I am asking you to reframe your thoughts before judging me. To accept my failings as a political inevitability. I didn't fail because I was a dog. Rather, I failed despite being a dog. What I mean is that anyone would have failed in my position. Because none of the politicians had a clue what they were doing either. They were just making it all up as they went along. It was a surreal few years of chaos that showed no sign of ending. There was nothing the political class could do about it.

There was no sense of mystery left to government. In calmer times, governments just get on with managing the economy and whatever else needs doing and most people only intermittently pay any attention. They are too busy getting on with their own lives and they have a basic belief that politicians will more or less try to do the right thing. Now the public couldn't take their gaze off the politicians. People had rightly lost faith in their leaders. That magical thread had been severed. The political class had been stripped naked and all that was on show was their ineffectiveness and vulnerability. It was clear that no one had any idea how to make Brexit work. Remainers were furious that their worst fears had been realised. Leavers indignant that something they had been promised would be simple was proving to be anything but.

Chaos had become endemic in government. Almost nothing worked as it should. If I was looking for a personal success story, all I could come up with was my own survival. Countless politicians and hangers-on had fallen by the wayside, but I was still there. Doing my bit for the country. Or not. Because crisis brings its own stasis.

We were all working silly hours. I would often be in by eight in the morning – something that drove Jill and John mad as it meant I had to take them for their walk at about six – and I wouldn't leave until well after seven. Others got in even earlier to hear the latest disaster on the morning's radio and TV round, where some hapless minister would be unable to explain what precisely was going on. It wasn't their fault they didn't know. No one did. Not that I ever felt sorry for them. They should have known what they were letting themselves in for when they took the job. But that's the vanity of politicians for you. They all think they will be the one to buck the system. Whose career won't end in failure.

Every week was much the same. I would get home knackered on a Friday evening, look back at what I had done and conclude that I had achieved next to nothing. Not just me. All of us. Because most of what I was doing – I had rather given up on briefing Labour on the government's Brexit plans because that took about five minutes a month – was being busy getting nowhere. Much ado about nothing. Answering endless phone calls from reporters desperate for a story on the latest Brexit developments and having to explain that nothing having changed was a sign of great progress. Doing the same with junior ministers and backbenchers desperate for something to tell their constituents. Sometimes we disappeared so far through the looking glass that what we were briefed to say in the morning was no longer true by the afternoon. And vice versa. This kind of thing gets exhausting after a while, I promise you.

But things were about to change for me. In a way I hadn't foreseen. It began with the exit of Nick and Fi. Someone had to take the blame for the disastrous election result and it sure as hell wasn't going to be

Theresa. I can't say I was sorry to see them go. I was sure they would soon find some other people to shout at. They were good at that. In their place came Gavin Barwell and Robbie Gibb. I never had much contact with Robbie but Gavin was a total darling. He had lost his seat as an MP at the election and was just thrilled to be back in the centre of the action. There was an air of straightforward hopelessness about him that charmed everyone. A genuine beta male. Best of all, he was a good judge of a dog. He knew how to get the best out of me. Unfailingly polite. I appreciated that. You could just tell he was destined to end up in the House of Lords within a matter of years.

Theresa, though, was in freefall. We had all hoped that the summer recess might do her some good. That walking in the Alps with her husband would have cleared her mind. Lifted her depression and provided some clarity over the likely best next steps. Only she came back in a worse state than ever. Barely able to string a sentence together and stuck in denial. Ask her how she was feeling and she would croak that the election had been a stunning success. It was embarrassing. She would even do it during prime minister's questions. Losing her majority was all part of the plan to deliver the best possible Brexit.

Everyone in Number 10 was at their wit's end. One Friday evening, Gavin slid up to my desk with a half-empty bottle of wine.

'You don't, do you?' he asked. Typical Gav. Always a gentleman even when he was a bit pissed.

'No,' I replied. 'But do carry on. You look as if you need it.'

'You're not wrong.'

'So, what's up?'

'I just can't get through to the PM any more.'

'You mean, you could once?'

'Well . . . Yes . . . Sort of . . . I mean, relatively speaking. Obviously she was never a great conversationalist. Unless you're a fan of early AI. But you could more or less communicate with her. Now, she's just shut down . . .'

'Maybe you should reboot her.'

'It's not funny. I will go in for meetings with her and I will talk for ten minutes about the agenda for the coming days and she will just stare at me blankly and say nothing. I will say, 'Is this OK with you?' and she will give a half-smile and a nod. You think the message has got through. Only you will then find the next day that she hadn't taken in a word and has done something completely different. It's making government impossible.'

Gav necked his glass.

'So, I've got an idea,' he continued. 'How about you try and get through to her? Perhaps you can achieve what I can't. You have the advantage of being a dog. Obviously a very special dog, but a dog nonetheless. You might stand out a bit as a Number 10 staffer, but you're also somehow invisible. To many people you are just a dog. An unthreatening cockapoo. You make most people feel good about themselves. And you could do the same for Theresa. Just go and lie in her office. Pretend you've dropped in for a snooze. And then, when you think her guard is down, when she's thoroughly relaxed, you can engage her in conversation. It would be far better than me hovering for the right moment that never came.'

I could see he had a point. It might just work. And it wasn't as if I was that busy. Neither Brexit nor the Labour Party were going anywhere anytime soon.

'It's a deal,' I said.

'Legend,' he replied, giving me a friendly pat on the head.

Thereafter, I would spend the first part of my mornings at my desk, dealing with any problems, and for the rest of the day I would just hang around Theresa's office. Curl up in a corner somewhere and try to blend in. Waiting until the prime minister's guard was down. Except it never really was down. There were moments when she looked slightly more relaxed and I would offer up a gentle, 'How are you feeling?' and then the shutters would come down immediately. There was nothing aggressive about this. She didn't appear angry that I had spoken. Our silences were entirely companionable. I even think she enjoyed having me in the room. She just wasn't capable of conversation. She had reverted to a pre-verbal state.

After a while, it became apparent to me that the only things with which she was entirely comfortable were the two pot plants on her desk. They were the only living things with which she seemed to empathise. She would make a point of watering them each day and pruning any dead leaves. And when she thought I might be asleep, I could occasionally hear her whispering to them. 'Is it safe? Is it safe?' Like out of the movie *Marathon Man*. This was the closest Theresa would ever get to therapy. There again, I wasn't about to suggest she went to see Caroline.

Touchingly, both pot plants attempted to reach out to her. They would lean in to reassure her. I could hear them say to Theresa that everything was going to be OK. And just for that moment, she appeared to be at peace with herself. That was the closest to physical contact she could manage. Gavin was amazed when I told him. He even arranged a meeting with me and the pot plants.

'How do you think she is doing?' he asked.

'You've got to realise she's a badly damaged woman,' said Pot Plant One. 'There's a lot of unresolved trauma.'

'To put it bluntly, she's a mess,' added Pot Plant Two. 'She's really hard work.'

Pot Plant Two always was a bit of a gobshite.

'I think we're containing her,' said Pot Plant One. 'But she's still very fragile.'

Gavin paused for a while. Thinking. Eventually he spoke.

'Then here's what we do. From now on, the pot plants go with Theresa everywhere. The future of the country depends upon them. And you, Herbie, can be the plants' minder. Make sure they have everything they need.'

Which is how, a few days later, I found myself sitting next to the two pot plants flying to Italy. Trying to stop Pot Plant Two from having a third gin and tonic. Everyone had thought it would be a good idea to get Theresa out of herself a bit. So, Number 10 had hired the Santa Maria Novella – a beautiful palazzo in Florence – for the day and invited the British media and some EU bods to hear Theresa give a talk on her latest thoughts on Brexit.

It turned out that trying to prevent Pot Plant Two from getting pissed was the least of my troubles. For reasons best known to himself, Robbie G had decided to come to the spiritual home of the Renaissance only to cover up the frescoes with a large backdrop that said, 'Shared History. Shared Challenges. Shared Future'. We could literally have been anywhere. We might as well have stayed at home.

The speech itself was a total disaster because, if there was to be a shared future, Theresa was in no mood to let anyone in on it. She just burbled aimlessly about Brexit meaning Brexit. Unwittingly, she seemed to be making a better case for the UK remaining in the EU than for leaving it. Her unconscious at work. Still, she did make some kind of history. Normally, she lost an audience within five minutes. Now she had lost it in two. Florence and the Machine. I did suggest to everyone that we might drop in to the Uffizi gallery on the way back, so we got something positive out of the day. Gavin nipped that one in the bud. I didn't even try to stop Pot Plant Two getting hammered on the way home. You only live once. And, by and large, the life of a pot plant is quite limited.

Bizarrely, Theresa thought the Florence speech had been yet another Brexit success story. Gav didn't seem to be in the mood to disabuse her. He was too busy concentrating on her leader's speech at the upcoming Tory party conference. This was an occasion she just had to nail. To convince the doubters in her party she did have a plan and that she was the person to deliver it.

Where to start? With the comedian Simon Brodkin who had managed to get into the Manchester conference centre and made his way to the stage to deliver a P45 to Theresa? Which Theresa only went and accepted. Because deep down that's what she wanted. To be out of a job. With the prolonged coughing fit that followed? One that got so bad that Theresa could barely speak for five minutes. And could only offer a hollow rasp for the rest of the speech. Most people in the audience could barely bring themselves to watch. It felt like intruding on a private grief. Just when you thought Theresa might just about make it to the end, the letters on the backdrop started falling to the floor in the heat. Or maybe it was the frog leaping out of her throat to cause havoc behind her. Theresa's world had literally fallen apart.

The atmosphere backstage afterwards was excruciating. None of us could bear to look Theresa in the eye. Gavin didn't even bother to say that it hadn't been that bad, because it so obviously had. Theresa just stood there motionless. Reliving the horror. One by one we all tiptoed out of the room. Just before I left, I looked round to see Theresa kneeling in front of Pot Plant One. A large tear fell from her eye onto one of his leaves. Pot Plant Two just gave me a wide grin.

I think that was the moment when we all recognised the game was up. That however long Theresa hung on, there was no coming back. She was finished. You might think that I have exaggerated all this for comic effect and pathos. But I really haven't. This is exactly how it felt to be in government at this time. You might also think I had become unnecessarily cynical now that I was a middle-aged seven-year-old. Possibly that's true. No one could have spent as long as I had in Westminster through such turbulent times without becoming a bit jaded. If you were away from your phone for an hour, you were in danger of missing something. You could get through three news cycles in an afternoon. It was exhausting.

Don't worry. I'm not about to go through every twist and turn in the Brexit negotiations here. For one thing, most of them turned out to count for nothing and for another they've been thoroughly chronicled elsewhere. Besides which, I wasn't really party to many of them. More a curious observer. But what I would like to do is to give a sense of the occasion. To convey just how abnormal things became. Most of the country wrote this off as a Westminster soap opera. Yet it was worse, much worse than that. More a horror film with real-life consequences for people.

Some politicians just enjoyed the drama. Others were complicit with their lies. Theresa just sleep-walked through it. This was seriously not OK. What we had was weird people behaving weirdly.

Things fall apart. Ministers began to fall like nine-pins. So much so that it began to feel disappointing when there hadn't been a resignation or a sacking for a few months. Defence secretary Michael Fallon had to go when various people started complaining about his unwanted sexual advances. Thank God, he had never tried it on with me. I've never bitten anyone but for that I would have had to make an exception. Minister for the cabinet office Damian Green turned out to have been spending most of his time watching porn on his computer. Though he claimed to have no idea how the porn got there. God works in mysterious ways. Most bizarrely of all, international trade secretary Priti Patel turned out to have been freelancing as foreign secretary by drawing up her own agreements with Israel. We all had fun checking her homeward flight, counting down the hours till she got sacked.

No one seemed to be doing the job they were supposed to be. Take Brexit secretary David Davis. Now, I quite liked David. In private, he was a bit of a laugh and I admired the way he stood up for free speech. He was one of my biggest supporters in Downing Street. 'Let the dog speak,' he used to say. 'Herbie has as much right to be heard as any of us.' So, a good egg. But David had one major drawback. He was actually quite lazy. Or perhaps a kinder way of putting it was that he was naturally disposed to think that everything would turn out just fine one way or another. Given the choice between hard graft and chatting to mates over a glass or two of wine, then the vino won every time.

It was just unfortunate that everyone was looking to David to provide the country with some guidance over Brexit. In particular, he was supposed to have come up with fifty-seven different analyses of various sectors of the British economy. But whenever anyone asked him about them, he would come over all vague. Everything was fine, he used to say. Nothing to see there. By now, I was in contact with Hilary Benn, Labour's shadow Brexit secretary, and I emailed to let him know that we all had serious doubts over whether these analyses existed. Hilary tried to use parliamentary procedure to get David to publish them. Sure enough, they all turned out to be little more than Post-it notes. Embarrassing really.

The months rolled by as we all lurched from one crisis to the next. Brexit seemed to have rendered supposedly very bright people into halfwits. None more so than Theresa, who finally announced in the summer of 2018 that she had come up with a plan. She made a rare appearance in the Number 10 staff office to fill us in on the details.

'Here's what's going to happen,' she said. There was even a rare hint of excitement in her voice. She genuinely believed she was on the verge of a breakthrough. 'I'm going to summon the entire cabinet to Chequers at the weekend. And when they arrive, I'm going to make sure that everyone hands over their ministerial phones so they can't brief their pet journalists on what's happening.

'I'm then going to reveal my plan to them and insist that everyone signs up to it there and then. Anyone who doesn't will be sacked on the spot. For them there will be no ministerial car to take them back to London. They will have to call a cab or walk. And your job is to be my eyes and ears. To listen in on private conversations to make sure no one is plotting behind my back or has brought a burner phone with them.'

A few days later, a dozen or so of us piled into a minibus outside Number 10 to take us up to Chequers. On arrival, I was feeling peckish, so I headed into the kitchen and persuaded the cooks to give me a sausage roll. I can be very charming when I want to be. Then to work. To check out the house and grounds and await the arrival of the cabinet. Late morning, the cars began to roll up the drive and by lunchtime everyone was assembled in the living room.

Theresa got to work. Her plan was actually very simple. And entirely impractical. She proposed to keep the bits of the single market and the customs union that she thought might be beneficial to the UK and to ditch the rest. A child could have spotted the obvious flaw that there wasn't a cat in hell's chance of the EU allowing us to cherry-pick the bits we wanted. It was either all or nothing. But by this stage in the negotiations, the cabinet was too brain-dead to raise any real objections. Most just wanted a nice day out in the country and a ride home in a ministerial car. No one was there to rock the boat.

Still, no one was really prepared to commit themselves. Instead, there was a lot of, 'This is very impressive, prime minister. A major step forward.' Most were just waiting to hear what Boris Johnson had to say. Only Boris, too, was reserving judgement. Until, later in the evening, he banged his fist on the table.

'This is a masterpiece, Theresa,' he declared. 'This is the real Brexit the country deserves. Congratulations. I'm behind you every step of the way.'

I leant over to Pot Plant One and whispered, 'I bet you a fiver that means he resigns by the end of the weekend.'

'Cynic,' he replied.

As it happened, I was out by a day. Boris didn't resign until the Monday. And then only after David Davis had done so first. For David, I think it was just all too much. He had realised the Chequers plan was dead on arrival and just couldn't face the hard slog of trying to come up with something that would be acceptable to both the warring factions of the Tory party and the EU. Far easier just to escape, claiming the moral high ground.

As for Boris, he resigned because he was always going to. He couldn't help himself. David jumping ship was like a trigger for him. A reminder to play the disloyalty card. He had no idea what a Brexit deal would look like. Nor much interest in finding a solution at this point. All that mattered was rolling the pitch for himself. Anything to make Theresa's life as miserable as possible. It must be so tiring, so lonely to be Boris. Knowing that any friendship – any close relationship – is only skin-deep. That there is nothing or no one who can't be sacrificed on the altar of his self-gratification. Even the worst dogs I've met – and I've met a few unpleasant types at Canines Anonymous – have more scruples than Boris. He doesn't even care if his venality and dishonesty is completely exposed. He goes naked into this world. His need to be the centre of attention is all he truly has.

The final year of Theresa's time in office passed in something of a blur. I think I must have managed to blank most of it out. My therapist, Liz, says that's sometimes the best way. There are some wounds that are just too deep. The skill is to resist re-enacting the trauma so it doesn't inform the rest of your life. Even though I was never that close to Theresa and certainly never shared her politics, there was something intimately painful about being so close to her decline. She knew and we knew that her time in Number 10 could only end one way, but we colluded with her to let her think she just might survive.

The EU rejected her deal as they were always going to. More than that, they continued to humiliate her in Brussels by treating her as an unwanted toy. Someone to be taunted and discarded. The UK would never be forgiven for Brexit. Nor was it just the EU who treated her badly. It was her own party, too.

Engaged in a brutal civil war. Brexiteers furious that the Thousand Year Brexit – The One True Brexit – was not being delivered. Remainers equally angry that the country's future was being dictated by a hardcore of right-wingers and the Northern Irish Democratic Unionist Party. The Labour Party often felt no more than ghosts at her funeral.

Come 2019 and we were down to the last rites. Endless arguments on how to settle the Northern Ireland problem. I kept my mouth shut through this one. There wouldn't be any thanks for the dog who pointed out the obvious – that there was always going to be a contradiction between leaving the single market and preserving the open borders between Northern Ireland and Ireland that had been enshrined in the Good Friday peace agreement.

Tory MPs argued long and hard over this and got nowhere. One morning, while I was keeping Theresa company in her office, a junior minister called Kit Malthouse came rushing in to Number 10, demanding to see the prime minister.

'I've cracked it,' he said. 'I've reached a compromise.'

'Go on,' replied Theresa.

'It's like this. We just pretend that we've come up with a plan that reconciles leaving the single market with the Good Friday Agreement. What we'll do is imagine that one day we will have brand new technologies that can double as both a border and not a border.'

'I see. And what do we do until then?'

'Nothing. Nothing at all.'

I couldn't believe what I was hearing. I was just waiting for Theresa to start laughing. To suggest that Kit got help for his dangerous fantasies.

Instead.

'That's totally brilliant,' she said. 'Let's give it a try.'

This may have been the moment Theresa's last grip on reality loosened. Things rapidly deteriorated. The Tory fighting, both in and out of parliament, was brutal. Theresa could barely buy a vote. In the European elections, the Tories ended up on 9 per cent of the vote with Nigel Farage's new Brexit Party way out in front. People preferred Nige's dishonesty to Theresa's incompetence.

Theresa was falling apart. I hadn't been allowed in to see her for a while – things were that bad – but when I did get to have a look inside her office again, I was shocked by what I found. Pot Plant One had wilted badly. His soil almost completely dried out.

'What's up?' I asked, tipping a glass of water into his saucer.

Pot Plant One could barely manage a whisper.

'She's . . . just . . . given up . . . on me . . . Hasn't . . . fed me . . . for more than a week . . . She doesn't . . . speak to me . . . Only . . . stares . . .'

I picked up Pot Plant One and took him downstairs to my desk. All but one of his desiccated leaves fell off. He was barely even a stem. For the next few days, I put him in intensive care. Feeding him, watering him.

Giving him sunlight. To no avail. He never spoke again and died later that week. I'm not sure if Theresa even noticed he had gone.

The letters of no confidence in Theresa had been mounting steadily so it was no surprise when the chairman of the 1922 Committee called a press conference to announce the threshold had been reached. Theresa was adamant she would fight on, but these words were just a Pavlovian response to danger. She was done. Finished. As were we all. Brexit had just claimed its latest victims.

Theresa was in tears as she made her resignation speech outside Downing Street. The press merely wanted to know what would happen next. Though deep down, we all knew. There was one surprise, though. Just before Theresa left Number 10 for the last time, she came down to find me at my desk.

'I want to give you this,' she said, handing over a bone. 'I know we haven't always seen eye to eye, but you've been a loyal dog. You've always been straightforward with me. Never soft-soaped or smooth-talked me. I appreciate that.'

At the very last, Theresa had revealed her humanity. Out of the corner of my eye, I caught sight of Larry sharpening his claws by the doorpost.

'Too soon, Lazza, too soon,' I mouthed. 'Give it another day.'

Larry shrugged. Whatever.

Chapter 12

I knew exactly how this was going to end. We all did.

It was one of the most predictable Tory leadership contests ever. This was Boris Johnson's time. Most Conservative MPs were fed up with the Brexit wars and just wanted someone to tell them that everything was going to be OK. They didn't care if it was mainly fiction, they needed someone in whom they could believe. Even if that person was a proven liar. Someone unable to publicly say how many children he had. Much like my own dad. I wouldn't be surprised if Brian had nudged his way into triple figures. And he's forgotten every one.

You'd have thought that might have disqualified Boris, what with the Tories claiming to be the party of family values. But if anything, his lies only made him more lovable to many people. Faults that would have brought down almost any other politician only added

to his charm. Everyone knew he was a blagger. That Brexit had only been an affectation for him. A pose to adopt to enhance his own political career. And three years on it had paid off. He was within touching distance of the crown. His own destiny fulfilled.

All that stood in his way was Jeremy Hunt. Which is to say that nothing stood in his way. Even Theresa May could have beaten Jeremy. So, in late July 2019, Boris duly became the latest incumbent in Downing Street. What no one had foreseen was that he would bring with him Dominic Cummings. A man not nearly as bright as he thought he was, but clever enough to have told Boris what to do during the Vote Leave referendum campaign.

Dom turned up for work in a T-shirt, hoodie and tracksuit bottoms and on his first day barged his way into our office.

'Good news, fucktards,' he said in his too-cool-for-school monotone. 'You're all fired.'

This came as no surprise. We had all guessed the writing was on the wall. New regime, new staff. We had all packed up our belongings the day before. But we had hoped our dismissal might have been a little more gracious. A kind of 'thanks but no thanks' parting message. Various people started leaving.

'That includes you, dog,' said Dom. 'Don't imagine you can hang around like you did last time. I'm personally walking you out the fucking door.'

His tone grated. Yet another posh boy with a sense of entitlement.

'I thought you wanted misfits and weirdos. What could be more of a misfit and a weirdo than a dog?' I replied.

There was a pause. Then, 'Just fuck off.'

'I see. You only want weirdos and misfits who went to Oxford and married into the aristocracy, then.'

I don't know where this sudden bravado had come from. Partly rage at being treated like this. Partly being demob happy. Knowing that there would be no come-back. That this was the end of my political career. Sign off on a high. This was too much for Dom. He picked me up and marched towards the front door. I caught sight of Larry on the way past.

'Bye,' I said.

'See you, Herbie. Stay in touch.'

'Now fuck off and stay fucked off,' snarled Dom as he dropped me. I shook out my fur and walked towards the security gates, hoping that none of the press snappers had caught my embarrassment.

Back home, I curled up on a cushion and had a long nap. It was time to take stock. I was now almost eight years old. Well into middle age. Not quite as old as John and Jill but not far off. I had had a good run in Westminster. The sort of career that many people would kill for. Dogs, too. But what to do next? I wasn't yet ready to retire. Most of my Downing Street colleagues would probably end up with a cushy lobbying job. Or maybe a handful of non-executive directorships. A couple of days' work a month for £50K. Somehow, I didn't see that happening to me. The wrong kind of dog. Not Tory enough.

Still, all that could come later, I decided. For now, I would give myself six months off. I needed to recover. Working on Brexit for the last three years had left me feeling jaded. All the arguments. All the lies. Never allowed to admit that no one had ever given a moment's thought to how it might work out. Now was the time for me to go all Gwyneth Paltrow. To indulge myself with the things I enjoyed doing. I would go to America with John and Jill to see Anna. Providing Donald Trump let me into the country. I would go to more opera. Read more books. Go for more walks. Meet up with all the dogs at my Canines Anonymous meetings, whom I had rather neglected.

So that's what I did. And I loved it all. For the first time in years, I felt thoroughly relaxed. Mind you, I didn't drop my interest in politics entirely. I kept track of what was going on in Westminster. The ongoing Brexit fights, the illegal prorogation of parliament and the snap election. Part of me missed being on the inside but I was also relieved not to feel strung out by it. To look at it more as theatre than as a conscious lifestyle. And I was certainly pleased to be well out of the election campaign. The nonsense slogan of 'Get Brexit Done', which duped a lot of the country. I think most people were just sick to death of it all and were ready to accept anyone who claimed to have an answer. They didn't even stop to think that the Northern Ireland Protocol had been negotiated by

David 'Frosty the No Man' Frost, one of the country's leading halfwits. They just wanted an end to it.

They certainly didn't want Jeremy Corbyn. Hell, I didn't want Jezza either. One lunch with him was more than enough for me to know he shouldn't be allowed anywhere near Downing Street. Even so, I won't deny I felt depressed when Boris won an eighty-seat majority. Allowing a narcissist the freedom to do whatever he wants is never the sign of a healthy democracy. Surely, even he couldn't screw this one up. Ten years of Boris just felt grim. At this rate, I would be dead long before there was even a chance of a Labour government. If that felt like a long time for you, then imagine how long it felt to me. I would have spent my entire life under one of the worst Tory governments of all time. And into the bargain, Spurs wouldn't even have won a Carabao Cup. That's what I call suffering.

Mostly, though, I needed time to reconnect with myself. Nice as it was to be spending time with John and Jill, their conversation is often a bit limited. Mostly they restricted themselves to saying 'walkies', 'din dins' and 'good boy' when I was around. Hardly that stimulating. It would have been nice to have occasionally talked about the state of the world. Or even the state of their bedroom. Clothes all over the place. To be fair, the semi-detachment was largely my fault. I realised I had become something of an observer of my own life. A bystander as the abnormal was normalised. I don't think I was alone in this. None of us could have survived with our sanity more or less intact without mentally absenting ourselves from the Brexit chaos. I'm still not sure if we were just unlucky to be governed by idiots at this time in our history or whether events would have made halfwits of anyone.

No matter. I was quite happy to be well out of it. Until one morning during a regular meeting of Canines Anonymous on the common, who should walk in but a Jack Russell cross. 'I'm Dilyn and I'm an addict,' he said. Now, I know these meetings are – as the name suggests – meant to be anonymous, but it goes without saying that we all instantly recognised him. How could we not? He was probably one of the best-known dogs in the country. The pooch that had taken up residence with the prime minister.

I'm not proud of this, but I took an instant dislike to Dilyn. I hated his newly acquired posh Notting Hill bark. He just seemed a bit too cocky. Too pleased with himself. Newcomers are meant to be shy and nervous. Find it difficult to speak and like to sit near the back. Dilyn had no such reservations. He was disarmingly eloquent. Happy to tell us all how he had been brought up on a puppy farm and had almost been executed for having the wrong sort of jaw. How he had been taken in by some rescue humans before picking out Boris and Carrie as his cohabitees. The poor dog made good.

If I'm honest, I was a bit envious. My addiction story wasn't nearly as exciting as his. My early life had been boringly cosy and middle-class, and my worst addiction was my anhedonia. The inability to enjoy things as much as I should. Also, my nose was put out of joint. I was used to being the celebrity dog at this meeting. The one who had held down important jobs. Had stories to tell. And now Dilyn had swanned in and was the centre of attention, with all the other dogs trying to pretend they didn't know who he was – 'Oh Dilyn, how interesting' – while hanging on his every word. I did the opposite, which was just as bad. I blanked him completely.

But Dilyn had a way of getting under your skin. He may have looked like the sort of dog who would turn up once and never be seen again, but he kept coming back. Twice a week. Regular as clockwork. And he joined in after the meeting when we would all go off to the cafe and try and grab stray chips and corners of bacon sandwiches that had been dropped. After a month or so, he took me completely by surprise by nudging me to one corner and asking me to be his sponsor.

'I like your recovery,' he said. 'I like the way you talk about your humans. Plus, you know how weird Number 10 can be. You've been around a bit and I think there's a lot I can learn from you.'

I felt ridiculously flattered. Even though I had been going to meetings on and off for years, no dog had ever asked me this before. I had begun to wonder if that was because I made everything look so depressing. Or, if what I had to offer, no one wanted.

'Er . . . OK,' I replied. What else was I going to say? 'I'm not a big one on working the steps. But if you just want someone to talk to about whatever is going on in your life, then I think it could work.'

'That's exactly what I want.'

We swapped phone numbers and emails and agreed that he should keep in contact every other day. Even if there was nothing much going on, it would be good to know how he was feeling. In truth, I think I was a rubbish sponsor because we ended up more like friends, which isn't quite the way these relationships are supposed to work. I even got to tolerate his bark. The thing is though, there was, despite his affectations, something quite endearing about him. Perhaps it was his vulnerability and honesty that I responded to. He was also – and this is rare in an addict – quite without self-pity.

He never tried to make a drama out of his upbringing on the puppy farm. Nor did he minimise the damage it had done to him. Like all dogs, he had separation issues, but he got by the best he could. His real anger was reserved for Boris and Carrie. They might mean well but they were just babies. Incapable of looking after themselves, let alone anyone else. Endless screaming matches as Boris would get pissed and spill wine all over the sofa. On one occasion things had got so bad, Dilyn had even had to call the police.

Then there was the mess. I might have thought John and Jill were slobs but they were nothing on Boris and Carrie. Dilyn had even tried doing a dirty protest in an attempt to get them to notice but they just left it where it was. In the end, Dilyn was so disgusted, he had to clear up his own shit. He never pulled that stunt again. He even reckoned that if they weren't so posh and rich and were living in a council house then any children they had would have been taken into care. For all that, Dilyn did have an innate loyalty. He never once sought to get Carrie and Boris rehomed. Perhaps he was just codependent. And he did admit to me that he quite liked being one of the most photographed dogs in the country. So he was there for the duration.

Come the new year of 2020, everything got rather more serious. I first started hearing about the coronavirus on the news in January. Back then, it was just some new infectious disease that we all thought would be contained to the Far East. But through February and into early March, it became clear the virus was going global. The scenes from northern Italy of villages isolated and lone mourners at funerals were horrific. And it was clear the virus was heading to the UK. Not just a few cases but as a pandemic. At least it was obvious to me. And Jill and John.

But not, apparently, to Boris. Dilyn was at his wits' end.

'He just doesn't get it,' he said to me. 'He thinks it's all a bit of a joke. Like some kids' party infecting everyone with chickenpox. Boris doesn't realise that thousands of people are going to die. He has missed five COBRA meetings and has a laugh about shaking hands with Covid patients in hospital. At this rate, he is going to become the country's first superspreader.'

I nodded. It was exactly what I had feared.

'So this is where you come in,' Dilyn continued.

'Me? What the hell can I do?'

'I want you to come back and work in Downing Street. You've got experience of working with David Cameron and Theresa May, so you know all the ropes. The trouble with the Number 10 operation at the moment is that it's being run by a load of fantasists and ideologues. You wouldn't trust any of them to run a bath let alone a country. You're needed, Herbie.'

I shook my head. It wasn't just the ethics of being headhunted by my CA sponsee, it was Boris.

'I really don't think I can. I'm sorry to say this about your human, but you know how I feel anyway. Boris is a narcissist. Someone who can be unfailingly polite to your face and then fuck you over behind your back. Completely untrustworthy. His whole career has been about his self-glorification. He makes Theresa look statesmanlike.'

'I agree. I feel pretty much the same way. But that's precisely why you have to do it. This isn't about what you want or how you feel. This is about doing something for your country. You often talk about the importance of service in CA meetings. Well, now is the time for you to walk the walk. We know thousands, possibly hundreds of thousands are going to die. If you come on board as Boris's point dog on Covid then maybe we can minimise the number of deaths. Your job is just to keep Boris focused on the coronavirus. Make sure he doesn't keep getting distracted. So, you will liaise with the cabinet and the senior medical advisers to make sure he follows directions.'

Put like that it was hard to refuse.

'OK,' I said. 'I'll do it. But how do we know Boris will agree? He hates anyone who reminds him that Brexit was an idiotic idea.'

'Well, just don't mention Brexit then. It's not as if anyone else is. Everyone in Number 10 is just saying it's done, even though it obviously isn't. Besides, this is all about Covid now. And don't worry about Boris. I've squared this one away with Carrie and Boris does everything she says. He's terrified of her.'

'Like he was terrified of Marina, Jennifer, Petronella or whoever else he was shagging . . .?'

'Just concentrate on Carrie. She's the boss now. For the time being at least. And don't forget that you and I have one other thing going for us. We're dogs. So, we can't get Covid. That means if the whole of the rest of the cabinet goes down with the virus, then we will be running the country. For the first time in years, it might actually work normally.'

So, just a few days later I was doing something I had never expected to do again. Walking through the Downing Street front door. Larry was the first to greet me.

'Didn't think I would see you again,' he said, putting a paw affectionately around my neck.

'Me neither. I've missed you, Larry,' I replied.

'I've missed you, too.'

Dominic Cummings appeared from a side room.

'What the fuck are you doing here? I thought I had fucking fired you,' he snapped.

'Well, I've just been fucking unfired. Now, if you will excuse me.'

I shoved my way past and showed myself up the stairs to Boris's study. The door was already open, so I walked in and climbed up on the chair opposite his desk.

'Good morning, Hubert,' he said.

'It's Herbert.'

'Sorry?'

'Herbert. I'm Herbert. But call me Herbie.'

'Yes, yes. Of course you are. That's what I meant. Now do sit down.'

'I already am.'

'So you are. May I say how pleased I am that you are coming back to work in Number 10. I've always been a huge admirer of yours . . .'

'Can we cut the flattery crap? I know you don't really know the first thing about me . . .'

'I'm sorry. I just can't help myself. I go on to bullshit autopilot. The cabinet seems to love it. But then they are all utterly useless.'

'Let's cut to the chase. I'm here to work with you on Covid. I don't trust you but, somehow, I'm going to get you to behave like an adult and we'll make this relationship work. Now, here's what's not going to happen. I'm not going to be taking any orders from

Dom. He can go and be unpleasant elsewhere. Nor will I have anything to do with cabinet secretary Simon Case as he's totally feeble. Can barely decide what socks to wear in the morning. This is the chain of command. I report to you. You report to Carrie. Carrie reports to Dilyn. Dilyn reports to me. Everyone's happy. Got it?'

'Got it.'

Having set up my own desk in the corner – near the window, obvs – of Boris's office, I went downstairs. There was one last thing to do. In my old office, I went looking for Pot Plant Two. I found him next to the printer looking somewhat the worse for wear.

'What took you so long?' he said.

'Oh, I dunno. This and that. Things to do.'

'Thank God you're back. It's only the cleaner who has been keeping me alive. If I'm lucky, I've been getting a glass of flat San Pellegrino once every two weeks. It's been hell. I'm bored out of my mind. No one says a word to me.'

'You surprise me.'

'Just Dom shouting about Bismarck and Ooda loops. There's something not right about that guy.'

'Tell me about it. Anyway, I'm pleased to see you.'

'You me, too.'

'You're safe now.'

I picked him up and took him up to my new office and put him on the window ledge. So that he would be able to look out. The A team was back in business.

Within days, the country was in lockdown. Cummings tried to claim it was all down to him but it wasn't. Dom has the unique gift of making people want to do the exact opposite of anything he suggests. So, if anything, he was the problem. Rather, it was a combination of me and the chief medical officer, Chris Whitty, forcing Boris to sit down and concentrate on the scientific data. Up till this point, Boris had had a mañana attitude. There was nothing that could be done today that couldn't just as well be done tomorrow. For a supposedly bright man, he had the concentration of a gnat. Getting up every five minutes or so to wander off and help himself to another chunk of cheese from the fridge. It got so bad that Chris and I had to lock the door and stand guard over him until he made a decision. Even then, he dithered about it being very un-Conservative to tell people to stay at home. I had to point out that I didn't think it was particularly Conservative to let thousands more people die unnecessarily.

It was sod's law that, not long after, Boris himself got Covid. Only a matter of time, really. He had never taken the risks to his own health seriously. He would go on TV explaining to the country what precautions everyone should take, only to ignore them all when he was off camera. I couldn't quite work him out. Partly, I think it was arrogance. He thought he was too important to get it. Not just that his position as prime minister gave him some kind of immunity but that being Boris Johnson set him apart. Behind that, though, was a vulnerability. A terror. The only way he could cope with the possibility of a serious illness was to make light of it. He was a complicated, badly damaged man. Most of the country only saw the jokey exterior. But inside, he was emotionally fragile. Unable to accept basic truths, desperate to be loved. A man with a large public ego but with no real sense of self-worth. In short, a mess. Hardly the kind of man you would want running the country during the worst public health crisis for one hundred years. Or even running the country in a time of calm. But the voters had decided otherwise.

Five days into Boris's illness, I started to get really worried. It was clear he was going downhill: his cough was worse and he was getting sweaty and breathless. But everyone else in Number 10 seemed relatively unconcerned. Happy to take Boris's assurances that he felt reasonably well and would be better soon.

Dilyn was doing his nut.

'He may be a twat,' he told me, 'but he's my twat. He could die. Look at the state of him. He's hardly healthy at the best of times.'

'Don't worry,' I said. Trying to sound more upbeat than I felt. 'I won't let it come to that.' And I didn't. But only just in the nick of time. When everyone else was wondering what to do, it was me who rang the hospital and got Boris taken into intensive care. Not that I'm looking for applause. I just did what any other dog would have done. But good to get the chance to put the record straight.

While Boris was in hospital and then away in Chequers recuperating, the country was being run by Dominic Raab. An even more terrifying prospect than it being run by Boris. Raab was quite the scariest man I have ever met. I had to vacate my desk in the prime minister's office while he was in charge because I just couldn't stand the tension. What is it about men called Dom? I've yet to meet one that isn't a psychopath. This Dom radiated repressed anger. He had a vein in his forehead that used to throb every time something displeased him. His silences were oppressive. If I didn't know better, I'd have assumed he had a sideline as a serial killer. A Mr Hyde alter ego who went on murderous sprees. Whose conscience wasn't even pricked when he looked out of the window the next morning to spot several bodies floating face down in the Thames. It was a massive relief when Boris came back to work a few weeks later. Words I thought I would never write.

Then Downing Street has always been full of strange characters. Men and women who became even stranger in stressful situations. And make no mistake, Covid was a stressful time. Everything about it seemed surreal. From walking in to work through near-deserted streets to getting to grips with a totally new and deadly illness. It felt as if we had time-travelled back to a mediaeval world where just the act of living was fraught with danger.

Having Matt Hancock as health secretary didn't do much to alleviate the stress. It was sod's law that Matt had chosen a global pandemic as the best moment to have a midlife crisis. Or maybe he was always like that. Right from the off, Matt was desperate to impress everyone. Even those who didn't count. He even used to boast about what he was doing to Pot Plant Two. He wasn't to know that Pot Plant Two was about the toughest audience you can get.

In less pressured times, Matt would have made for an interesting psychological case study. A man of seemingly little talent who had risen to become one of the most important figures in the government. As it was, he was just irritating. Quite the neediest man I've ever met.

'It's not fair,' he said to me once. 'I got Covid at the same time as Boris and no one cared if I lived or died.'

'That's because you're not prime minister,' I pointed out. 'And also because you didn't get it as badly as him.'

'But I could have done.'

'But you didn't. John and Jill got Covid, too, and they didn't make the news either. One of their friends actually died and he was just another statistic.'

'You do know that I was the first member of the government to become aware of Covid.'

'Really?'

'Yes. When I write my diary in two years' time, I'm going to reveal that I discovered the coronavirus in 2019.'

I fell silent. There was no arguing with this level of stupidity. But Matt wouldn't leave me in peace to get on with my work. It turned out that what he really wanted to talk about was his crush.

'Have you seen Gina?' he asked. 'I think she's really into me. We had a great snog by the photocopier.'

'I know. I've seen the CCTV footage.'

'I've written this great poem about her. Do you want to hear the first two lines?'

'No.'

'When Things are Getting Meaner
That's When I Need my Gina.'

Thank you and goodnight.

You might have thought that government would have had contingency plans for a pandemic. But what they did have was totally inadequate for the scale of the health crisis. Everyone was just making stuff up as they went along and it was my job to try and get Boris to sign off on the more sensible schemes. It was certainly an eye-opener. Take the furlough scheme to support businesses whose staff were unable to work. Normally, government and opposition parties go to war over £500 million of funding commitments. Where's the money coming from? How is it going to be paid for? Now, chancellor Rishi Sunak was going to find £70 billion and no one batted an eyelid. It made me realise that budgets aren't quite as fiscally tight as ministers suggest. When push comes to shove, governments can always find the money if they want to.

Which brings us to personal protective equipment or PPE. Or the lack of it. Doctors and nurses were having to make their own out of plastic bin bags. For cabinet minister Michael Gove, this wasn't a matter of national shame. It was a wonderful opportunity.

'Good news, Herbert,' he said, as he marched into my office one morning.

'Try me,' I replied.

'I've just started up this new scheme . . .'

'Weren't you supposed to run this past me first?'

'Must have slipped my mind.'

Mikey was looking even more shifty than usual and was sniffing loudly. He must have spent the previous night in the crack den on his department's roof rather than going home.

'Here's the thing,' he continued. 'The country is desperately short of PPE, so I'm now opening this new programme to invite members of the public to supply the government with masks, gloves and other healthcare supplies. Best of all there is a VIP lane for Tory party donors to get government contracts. You don't even have to pretend you know what you're doing as there's almost no vetting. It's a licence to make money. We've had all sorts of people who know nothing about PPE sign up already . . .'

'Don't tell me. Baroness Michelle Mone has already got a £100 million contract . . .'

'How did you guess? Anyway, the thing is that I'm inviting you, Jill and John to put in a tender. It's only right that those at the centre of government are the ones to profit in a crisis. If you can't be bothered to source PPE from factories in China, then just buy a load off Amazon and invoice my department for double what you have paid.'

'I think I'll pass,' I said. 'It somehow doesn't feel right.'

'Suit yourself. Was only trying to help.'

Most of my days were spent trying to prepare Boris for the daily 5 pm press conference, where the latest death totals were announced. It was a grim time and it took its toll on me. Just about the only good news we did get was that Dominic Cummings got Covid. I don't mean this unkindly. I didn't want anyone to get ill. But it was just such a relief to have him out of the building for three weeks. The mood in Number 10 lifted immediately. People stopped cowering behind their desks, afraid to say anything. There were even the odd smiles. People actually talked to one another. Shared ideas.

Typical Dom, though, to think that the rules didn't apply to him. That instead of self-isolating at his home in Islington he chose to go up to Durham instead. And then to get spotted going on a day trip with his family to Barnard Castle. What an embarrassment that was. Boris swore blind to me that he hadn't known but I didn't believe him. A liar is gonna lie. Inevitably, the media got wind of it and Dom gave one of his classically underwhelming press conferences in the Downing Street garden. Even when he is meant to be trying to be gracious, he drips with contempt. It was all a bit of a misunderstanding, he said. He had just gone for a drive to test his eyesight. An insult to his own intelligence as well as everyone else's. But Dom didn't care. Dom always got to do exactly what Dom wanted.

Dilyn and I watched all this from a nearby flower-bed. I was furious. Months of trying to get everyone to obey the rules undermined by Dom's exceptionalism.

'We've got to do something,' I said.

'We have,' Dilyn agreed. 'What do you suggest?'

'There's only one thing for it. You've got to work on Carrie. Tell her you'll walk out on the family if Boris doesn't sack him.'

'You think that will work?'

'It's worth a shot. Carrie dotes on you. She'll do anything for you.'

'OK. Let's go for it.'

That plan went on hold for a bit as I first had to try to stop Rishi Sunak from launching his daft 'Eat Out to Help Out' scheme. I failed. Eat Out to Kill Someone, more like. The levels of stupidity in Downing Street just notched up a gear.

But after the summer, Dilyn and I went into overdrive. Weird that two dogs who were in no danger of getting Covid were the ones who were doing the most to save the human population. I would drip, drip, drip-feed Boris with Dom's latest excesses. Who he had upset today. Why he wasn't needed. He always claimed he was the only one to understand the science. That he knew better than the scientists themselves. But Dom was right about one thing. Boris was like a broken shopping trolley careering this way and that. It was down to me to make sure I steered him more or less in the right direction.

Credit here to Dilyn. He did more than his fair share of the heavy lifting. He refused to be stroked by Carrie until she had persuaded Boris to fire Dom. Refused to accept any affection from her whatsoever. Come the autumn, Carrie cracked. Told Boris that it was her or Dom. That he would be the first prime minister to be forced to sleep in the car.

You wouldn't believe the mood in Downing Street on the day Dom was fired. Covid was temporarily forgotten. Everyone was ecstatic. No love lost. Dom raged and raged. Screaming that the country would be doomed without him as he packed up his belongings. Dilyn, Larry and I waited by the front door so that we could give him a send-off.

'Fuck off, you fucking fucktard.'

Chapter 13

It was only a little while ago, but I find it hard to recall the Covid years in any great detail. My memories are impressionistic. Snapshots of events rather than chronological accounts. Some things I have only been able to piece together through checking through my WhatsApp messages. I now regret not keeping a diary, though at the time it never occurred to me. By the time I got home each night, I was far too knackered to write. I just wanted to have something to eat, watch something mindless on TV and go to bed. I couldn't even muster any enthusiasm for curling up on the sofa at home.

And I can't guarantee that everything I write is entirely accurate. Boris Johnson's memories seem to differ significantly from everyone else's. And Matt Hancock's diaries suggest that the entire nation would have died without his interventions. But I am doing my best to be fair. To get as close to the truth as I can.

I know I am getting on a bit now but I am not in any way confused or forgetful. Especially compared to some other dogs I could mention. It's more that the Covid years were so stressful, so painful that the whole country has indulged in a form of collective denial. A national amnesia. We don't want to remind ourselves of what we endured and the choices we took. We just want to get on with our lives and forget the horrors. To ignore the fact that the past always informs our present. And nowhere is this more true than of those in government. They don't want you to remember the hundreds of thousands of graves. They want you to think of all the good things that lie ahead. Because that's the only way you would conceivably vote for them again.

This might sound odd, but I found the early days of the pandemic the easiest to deal with. Sure, there was a lot of scary stuff going on, including Boris's stay in intensive care, but there was a coming-together in Downing Street. Apart from when Dominic Cummings was involved. Petty feuds were by and large forgotten as we all tried to find a way of getting through the crisis. Much the same was going on across the country as a whole. Every Thursday at 8 pm I would find myself unexpectedly moved as people opened their front doors and began clapping for the NHS workers. There was a sense that everyone was looking out for one another.

But these good feelings didn't last more than a few months. I guess you can only survive on adrenaline for so long. Then it gradually dawned on us that there was going to be no quick fix. This wasn't a pandemic that would be all over in a matter of months. It would be years at least. Years of lockdowns, not being able to see friends and family and no real vision of what the world would look like when we did come out the other side. Of course, it wasn't all bad news. There was the day a vaccine was found. The day it was pronounced safe for use. The day Jill and John got jabbed. I hadn't seen them so happy for months. You could see the hope seep back. Most days, though, were just a struggle. Endless firefighting from morning to night. Living in the moment, not daring to think of a future. The daily death tolls in the thousands. Wondering when someone you knew would be the next statistic.

Then there was Boris. With me trying to be the conscience of a man whose first instinct was always to think of himself. Trying to get him to focus on the scientific data. So not his thing. Bizarrely, Boris thought of himself as Winston Churchill's natural successor. A man to lead the country in its time of crisis. But Boris was essentially frivolous. His empathy was always skin-deep. He would ask me how I was when I came into work in the morning but he didn't really want to know. He just wanted me to say that I was OK so he could carry on with what he was doing. And that was him in a nutshell. Desperate not to impose further lockdowns, even when he was told they were essential, because he didn't want to have to break the bad news to the nation that the pandemic was still out of control. He loved the trappings of power but not the responsibilities.

Did I like him? That's a trickier question to answer. Because he undoubtedly had something that most other politicians didn't. I've never met anyone who would want to spend more than twenty seconds with Dominic Raab. You'd need medication to deal with the rage. Same with Matt Hancock. Just completely self-obsessed. Not to mention deluded. As for Rishi Sunak, he would spend the first five minutes of any meeting telling you why you were lucky to spend time with him in person. But Boris did have a sense of fun. Could make you laugh against your better judgement. With him there was an illusion of intimacy.

Yet it was all only skin-deep. You can't have a proper relationship with someone who doesn't have a relationship with himself. Scratch the surface with Boris and all you found was his own solipsism. Everything was all about him. I suppose you could say that I should have used my position to call him out on all this. But I wasn't his therapist. So, I chose to take him as I found him. Trying to change him, to get him to understand himself, would have been pointless. I just laughed along at his gags and did my best to get him to concentrate on his job. That was hard enough work as it was.

You might wonder why I put myself through all this. Why I was so invested in helping the country through the Covid pandemic. Why I didn't just leave and spend my time in the park, safe in the knowledge that I was not in any personal danger from the disease. Well, for one thing, I had a sense of duty. Most dogs do. By and large, we are desperate to do the right thing. I worried for my humans. I didn't like to see them all stressed out the whole time. I didn't want them to get ill and die. Imagine having to find somewhere else to live at my age.

It was also a misconception that we dogs all had a good pandemic. Our humans at home all day with nothing to do but keep us company and be taken for walks. That was far from the truth. Even the humans we loved were nightmares during that two-year period. Extra needy. Constantly harassing us for reassurance. Wanting us to tell them that everything was going to be OK. Having them around 24/7 became rather trying. An interruption to our daily routines. We all need a bit of time to ourselves.

By far the worst, though, were those humans who couldn't bear each other's company on a sustained basis and went out and found a puppy to share their home. Very often that ended in disaster. Imagine being just a few weeks old and being responsible for keeping a human relationship together. Frequently, the strain was too much. The dog had a breakdown and so did the humans. Then there was the aftermath of the Covid pandemic with loads of humans deciding they couldn't be bothered with their mutts any more and kicking them out of the house. They had served their purpose and now were surplus to requirements. I can't tell you how many messed-up dogs I've met in the park who are under the impression that they are the ones who must have done something wrong. Not all were lucky enough to find new homes. Some were facing the death penalty. So, that's why I was invested in working to find an end to the pandemic. It was personal.

Somehow we muddled through. Just putting one paw in front of the other. Constantly fire-fighting. We reached the point where we planned for the opposite of whatever Boris had said would happen. When he repeatedly said there would be no third lockdown, we all knew what was in store for us. He even cancelled the daily 5 pm press conferences. Not because the country was fed up with them, but because he was.

Nor was there much else going on. Even Brexit was at a standstill. Perhaps no surprise, as David Frost, the man who had negotiated the final Brexit deal with the Northern Ireland protocol, had decided to rewrite history. The deal that he had proclaimed as a breakthrough back in 2020 and for which he had hoovered up a peerage, he now insisted had been rubbish all along. Hardly a great surprise, as everyone in Number 10 had long since concluded that Frosty was one of the dimmest people they had ever met. Larry used to openly laugh at him every time he saw him. Frosty wanted us all to believe that he had deliberately negotiated a deal that was unworkable and was now going to come up with a plan more to the UK's liking without anyone in the EU noticing. Needless to say, Boris was totally on board with this.

The biggest excitement of the early summer of 2021 was the resignation-before-he-was-sacked of Matt Hancock. Not so much for his affair with Gina becoming public knowledge – Boris was in no position to judge – but for breaking his own social-distancing rules. Weirdly, Matt seemed quite upbeat about breaking up his family when I bumped into him on the stairs after he had come to tell Boris he was resigning.

'We are finally free to be ourselves,' he said.

'How old are you?' I asked.

'Why do you ask?'

'Because you're acting like a fifteen-year-old.'

'We can now tell our truth.'

'Like snogging in the office.'

'We're in love. Have you ever been in love?'

No one had ever asked me that question before. Had I? I was unquestionably very fond of Jill and John. And Anna and Robbie too. Not to mention Mike, who came round once or twice a week to be taken out for a walk. It started as a public service on my part but has developed into something deeper. But did I love them? Maybe I did, but not in an obsessive kind of way. I missed them when they weren't around but I was frequently happiest in my own company. There was a strong attachment certainly, but one that was based on companionship. And there had never been another dog – either male or female – with whom I had ever wanted to settle down. Just loads of good mates, like Frida, with whom I liked to do things. Very often, I have found that the best friends are the ones you can choose to ignore for long periods with no hard feelings on either side. You just pick up where you left off when you see each other.

I chose not to answer Matt. Instead, I changed the subject.

'What do you plan to do next?' I asked.

'Not sure. A bit of reality TV would be nice.'

Was that his life's ambition? To appear on *I'm a Celeb*?

'Seriously?'

'Absolutely. Then I will write my Covid diaries.'

File them under fiction.

'Don't worry. I will make sure you get a mention.'

He didn't, of course.

'Goodbye then.'

'Goodbye.'

But then came my finest hour. It was early August when we first got wind that the Taliban was on the point of regaining control of Kabul. Needless to say, most of the cabinet were away on holiday. And Number 10 was down to skeleton staff. Some days, it was just me in the office and even I was slacking. Taking long lunch hours in the garden with Dilyn and Larry. Boris was his usual semi-detached self, seemingly unbothered about what was going on in Afghanistan. It was all a long way away and he had enough on his plate with Covid as it was.

'But we really need to get all the Afghans who have been working with us out of the country,' I said. 'Otherwise, they might get killed.'

'Do we?' Boris replied. 'I'm sure they will be fine. But you see what you can do if you like.'

So, it was rather left to me. I tried to mobilise Dominic Raab, the foreign secretary. He wasn't interested either. Three times my call went straight to voicemail. My WhatsApps went unanswered. Finally, though, he picked up.

'What do you want?' he asked.

I told him.

'Can't see there's any hurry,' he drawled. 'There's always more time than you think there is. Can you pass me the suncream?'

'What?'

'Sorry, I was talking to my wife. You wouldn't believe how hot it is here. Can't even go for a swim because the sea is closed.'

I had no idea what he was talking about. He must have had sunstroke.

'I think you need to come home,' I said.

'Well, tough. I'm staying put. Haven't had a proper holiday for months. If you're so bothered, then you deal with it.'

Defence secretary Ben Wallace was no more helpful. In fact, he was positively chippy. Hated the idea of me getting involved. 'I'm completely on top of this,' he said testily. 'Now bugger off and stop bothering me.'

Except he was clearly on top of nothing. You only had to switch on the TV to see that Kabul was in chaos. Thousands of people surrounding the airport desperate to get out and just a handful of British military personnel to control the operation. Almost no planes were getting out of Kabul even though Wallace claimed to have dozens on standby. It was heartbreaking. Some Afghans were so desperate they were storming the runway and hanging on to the outside of the planes. Many would have fallen to their death. All because no one in the UK government could organise a proper airlift. It was a betrayal of all those Afghans who had worked for us.

This got me thinking. If we couldn't get the Afghan people out, then maybe I could try and get the Afghan dogs out. Dogs who would be beaten and left to starve under the Taliban. Surely they, too, deserved a break. Time to get Dilyn on board.

'Here's the plan,' I said. 'We're going to rescue some dogs.'

'How about some cats as well?' said Larry.

'And some cats.'

'I can organise the plane, but I don't have anyone on the ground in Kabul who can round up all the animals. That's where you come in, Dilyn. I need you to ask Carrie if she knows anyone who can help. She's a sucker for a sad-looking mutt and has a lot of clout with animal charities.'

The next morning, Dilyn was waiting for me as I arrived for work.

'Sorted,' he said. 'Carrie is well up for this. She's even going to arrange homes for them all when they get back to the UK. The bloke you need in Kabul is someone called Pen Farthing. Ridiculous name, but there you go. Everyone says he's sound.'

Within hours it was all arranged. Pen replied to my WhatsApp immediately and promised to round up all the dogs and cats he could find. He would be waiting at the airport perimeter furthest from the main terminals at 11 am the following morning. Finding a plane was no bother. 'Just chartered a private plane and told them I had a slot booked for Kabul.' The aircrew had been hanging around for days waiting for something to do.

This was too good a trip to miss. I left the office, took a train and a cab to Stansted and in hours we were airborne. There was little chance for conversation as the crew didn't seem overly chatty, so I dozed fitfully for several hours behind the pilot's seat, only to be awakened as we made our steep descent into Kabul.

The heat and the dust were overpowering as the door of the plane opened and the steps lowered. Now the adrenaline began to kick in. There was no time to lose. Pen was waiting where we had agreed, along with a platoon of dogs and cats and sixty or so members of his staff. He shouted out some orders and they began boarding the plane in single file.

'Is that all of them?' I asked.

'Yup,' he said. 'There's ninety-four dogs and sixty-eight cats. I had hoped to evacuate more but there wasn't time.'

'That's fine. Now let's get out of here before anyone changes their mind and refuses to let us leave.'

The noise on the way back to the UK was indescribable. Every dog seemed to be shouting loudly though I couldn't understand a word any of them was saying as they were all barking in Pashto. Eventually a dog called Nowzad came and sat next to me. His English was near perfect and he told me that Pen was his human. This was a great day, he said. All the other dogs were merely saying how excited and grateful they were. They had thought they were going to be abandoned.

On our arrival back in Stansted, Carrie was there to greet us. She had been as good as her word and had provided accommodation for everyone. It was an emotional time. Every single dog and cat made a point of coming up to me and Dilyn to give us a hug and to say thank you. One even whispered that she would like to have my puppies. Thanks, but no thanks. There are enough absent fathers in the canine world as it is. She was attractive, though.

Nowzad was last to leave. Off to London with Pen.

'None of us will forget this,' he said.

'It was nothing,' I replied. 'Any dog would have done this.'

'That's where you are wrong.'

We sniffed each other's bums affectionately. 'Keep in touch,' I said. 'You know where to find me.'

That was the end of the gratitude. In Westminster, the shit was about to hit the fan. Ben Wallace was furious. How dare we arrange a flight just to rescue some mutts when there were so many other Afghans waiting to get out of Kabul? We should be ashamed of ourselves.

I was in no mood to back down. I was tired, grumpy and had had enough. There was no point in blaming me or Dilyn. Maybe the foreign office and the ministry of defence should check their own privilege. They should have seen the Taliban's advance on Kabul coming. There had been plenty of time to organise regular evacuation flights. Hell, if I could charter a plane at short notice to get a whole lot of dogs and cats out then why couldn't he?

'I'm going to have you sacked,' said Ben.

'Er . . . I don't think so. Carrie has my back. And Boris is terrified of upsetting her. I think you'll find it will be Dominic Raab who gets the sack. There again, he needs more time to wait for the sea to open.'

And that's more or less how it panned out. For me personally and for dogs and cats generally, the operation had been a triumph. Even Larry, the arch cynic, had a lump in his throat. I've had many disappointments, many career lows in my life, but I will always be able to look back on this success with pride. The one unequivocally good thing I have ever done. I had come into politics to make a difference. And, thanks to mine and Dilyn's efforts, there were now more than one hundred and fifty dogs and cats walking the streets who might otherwise be dead. It's a humbling thought. So, I must try not to get too big-headed.

Not that there's too much chance of that. Not while the elephant is still in the room. You might be wondering by now why I have spent so long writing about Boris and Covid without a single mention of parties. Truth is, I'm ashamed. Ashamed that I didn't do more to bring them to the public's attention sooner. Ashamed that so many of my colleagues, some of whom I counted as friends, were involved. Ashamed, too, that I even went to one of them. Ashamed that when so many people were making sacrifices to obey the social-distancing guidance, many of those in Number 10 – including the prime minister – thought the rules didn't apply to them.

Here's how I got involved. It was a hot, early summer's day in May. We had all been working flat out for weeks and were knackered. Then an email from Party Marty aka Martin Reynolds, the principal private secretary to the prime minister, dropped in everyone's inbox. We could all do with a break, he said. So, let's all meet up in the Number 10 garden that evening for socially distanced drinks. Bring your own booze. Typical Boris. Far too tight to fork out himself.

Perhaps I should have given it a second thought. Dozens of staffers did and declined. They didn't want to break the rules. But I didn't give it a second thought. I allowed myself to believe if the boss class had sanctioned it, then it must be OK. Sometimes I am too trusting for my own good. That evening, I came armed with a bottle of mineral water and started chatting to Dilyn in the flower bed. What followed shocked me. No one made an effort to socially distance. People were tucking into the food and booze, patting one another on the shoulder and, in some cases, hugging one another. Just as if lockdown had never happened.

I should have said something then and there, but I didn't want to be the one to rock the boat. Instead, I did nothing. Even though Number 10 cleaning staff were out in force the following day tidying up the bottles, no one mentioned the party again. Those who had declined the invitation said nothing. Those, like me, who went also said nothing. As if a complicit silence would absolve all guilt. It was the party that had never happened. Or was it even a party? Bizarrely, when the police came to investigate the parties eighteen months or so later, they concluded this wasn't a party. No one ever got a fixed penalty notice for it. Nor did the standards committee consider it. Perhaps I didn't go to a party after all. Perhaps I've been worrying unnecessarily. All I can say is that it sure looked like a party to me. But I'm getting ahead of myself here.

After the party that may not have been a party, I resolved to stick to the straight and narrow. How else could I look John and Jill in the eye? They were following the letter of the law even though it was damaging their mental health, so I should too. It wasn't always easy. Denial became the only survival mode. I would just go into work to do my job and leave. Made a point of keeping social activities to a minimum. Deleted any emails that weren't strictly work-related without reading them. Ignored the vomit in wastepaper baskets and bottles left lying round the downstairs office. Turned a blind eye to the sniggers when someone left with a suitcase via the back entrance to wander up to the Co-op near Trafalgar Square to restock the fridge with booze. Closed my ears to the gossip about who had copped off with whom. Said nothing when the deputy cabinet secretary, Helen MacNamara, turned up one day with a karaoke machine. Helen, of all people. A woman who often went out of her way to make sure we were all OK and coping. What was she thinking? What was I thinking? What were any of us thinking?

All of this took its toll on me. Canines Anonymous was supposed to be an honest programme. Its meetings a place where you could tell the truth without being judged. But I couldn't bring myself to say what was going on. Would just burble on about how stressful I was finding everything without saying what was really on my mind. It was the shame. The shame is the one thing that gets me every time.

But eventually something had to give. I wasn't sleeping properly and I felt as if I was falling apart. Now you might find this hard to believe but I hadn't even talked to Dilyn about this. Nor he to me. It was as if there was an omertà. Come the autumn of 2021, I decided something had to change. I sent him a WhatsApp. 'We need to talk urgently. In private.' He replied immediately. 'Sure. In the garden in five minutes . . .'

'I'm going mad,' I said.

'Tell me about it,' he replied. 'You try sharing a flat with Boris and Carrie and a baby.'

'It's about the lockdown parties. There's been so many of them. I can't keep quiet any longer.'

'You're right. I've been thinking much the same. I'm sure that Boris must know. You can't avoid the noise some nights. Rishi must also know. Unless he's stone deaf. Hell, there was even a party going on in the flat on the night Dominic Cummings got fired. Abba at full volume and plenty of booze. Don't tell me that's in the guidelines.'

'Are you sure you're OK with dobbing in your humans? There may be hell to pay.'

'I think so. Enough is enough. Just so long as it never emerges that it was me who grassed them up.'

'I was thinking the same. I'm just not that brave. Here's what I suggest. There's this schnauzer I vaguely know. Called Buddy. He lives in south London near me. Well, he shares a house with Pippa Crerar. The political editor of the *Mirror*. I could arrange a meet with him and he could pass on the story to Pippa. That might work.'

It took me a few days to track Buddy down, but once I had his phone number he quickly agreed to meet me. I pressed on him the need for secrecy. No problem, he said. Come to Dulwich Park on Saturday morning. I always take Pippa for a walk then. So, even if we are seen together, no one will think anything of it. Buddy had clearly done this sort of thing before. An old pro.

You never can keep the paranoia totally at bay. So, I insisted on arriving half an hour early to scout out the park. To check out there were no Number 10 goons watching me. No dogs trying just that bit too hard to act innocent. I took Joey and Frida with me to keep a lookout. I took them into my confidence and told them if they spotted anything they were to bark loudly.

Buddy hove into view. Turned out he had also been doing a recce and had concluded the coast was clear.

'Meet me behind the cafe in ten minutes,' he said. 'Best not to take any chances.'

'Gotcha.'

Once we were sure we were out of earshot I started talking. And didn't stop for the best part of half an hour. Talking him though all the different social gatherings and parties. Providing dates. Giving the names of everyone I believed to have been there.

'I've got all this down on a memory stick,' I added, handing it over to him.

'That's very helpful. Have we got photographs?'

'A few.'

'Excellent.'

'Now, you will promise to keep me and Dilyn out of it, won't you? And be sure to drip-feed the story bit by bit to keep it running for as long as possible.'

'I wasn't born yesterday.'

Over the next three or four months, Buddy and Pippa did us proud. No one even considered the possibility that I might have been implicated and the story consistently led the news. So much so that 'Partygate' was to become the thing that defined Boris's time in Number 10. No one was talking about how Brexit had been delivered. Largely because many of its supporters had lost faith in it. Even Covid and the lockdowns had been relegated to second place. Partygate was the only story in town. The fixed penalties that Boris and Rishi received and what they both knew.

The government was in meltdown. Just fire-fighting every day, issuing denials that they knew not to be true. It wasn't a great look for Boris or the country. And it was utterly dispiriting for me. I still wanted to believe there was some honour in government. Though even I could see the current bunch was morally bankrupt. A black hole into which anything good had been eaten up. It didn't do much for the self-worth of anyone working in Number 10, knowing that the whole country despised us. After believing that the parties were officially sanctioned, many in Westminster were now worried about their jobs and careers, thinking that they might never work in politics again. Worried that they were to be hung out to dry by politicians keen to save their own skins.

Boris was the worst. Naturally. Lying always had come easily to him and now he rewrote history with an alternative reality. Time and again he lied to parliament, the media and the country. What's more, we all knew he was lying. Even an accomplished sociopath like him must have known he was lying. Just as depressingly, almost all the Tory MPs sanctioned his lies. They knew he wasn't telling the truth, too, but they gave him their support. He was their man. What else could they do? Without him, they and the Conservative Party would be nothing. For me, it was especially galling. Having to sit opposite him in his office as he tried to gaslight the country. Maybe I should have called him out. Though it probably wouldn't have made any difference. Boris was hardly going to change now. So, instead, I chose to ignore him. Saying almost nothing unless spoken to. And then only 'yes or no' answers. I could tell my time in Number 10 was coming to an end. Covid wasn't a thing of the past yet but Covid Terror was. People were still dying but no one cared any more. No one even self-isolated if they got Covid. Almost everyone gave up testing themselves. It was as if the last two years had been a weird hallucination.

Boris's days in Number 10 were also numbered. His authority over the country was first to go. His authority over his party the last. But even Tory backbenchers got ground down by the drip drip of allegations and the ever more magical realism of the denials. Sometimes, the truth is hiding in plain sight. It wasn't Partygate that delivered the *coup de grâce* to Boris. It was his defence of Chris Pincher, a Tory MP who had been accused of sexual misconduct. This was the straw that broke the camel's back. Home secretary Sajid Javid and chancellor Rishi Sunak resigned in quick succession and that opened the floodgates for more than fifty other ministers to resign. Boris tried to ride it out for forty-eight hours but then, reluctantly and ungracefully, he gave his own resignation speech in Downing Street. In character to the last.

The following day, I sought out Dilyn.

'Are you OK?' I asked.

'I think so.'

'It's been brutal. I feel weird enough about having put the wheels in motion to topple a government. God knows how you must feel when it's the human you live with who has been forced to resign.'

'I'm coming to terms with it,' he said. 'You know what? I was never that happy being the dog who lived in Number 10. I felt cooped up. People came to think I was entitled and badly behaved when all I really wanted was the chance to be a real dog. To not have to share my home with hundreds of civil servants and politicians. Now I get my wish. Carrie has insisted we move to the countryside. Somewhere posh in the Cotswolds. So, I can run around fields to my heart's content. Boris will be fine, too. People like Boris always are. He's always moaned about being hard up as prime minister. Now he's going to be earning more than he could ever have imagined. £250K for the same badly prepared speech. What's not to like?'

'Put like that . . .'

'There's one other thing I've been meaning to ask you.'

'What's that?' I asked.

'It's . . . It's delicate. Carrie has negotiated with Boris to let me choose one person for his resignation honours list. And I would like to nominate you.'

'Me?'

'Yes. You. You've been a good friend and sponsor to me. You're one of the few people in this building to act with integrity. You saved the dogs . . .'

'And the cats,' Larry interrupted. I might have guessed that he would be listening in.

'And the cats,' said Dilyn. 'You also did more than anyone to expose the Partygate scandal. So, what do you say to a peerage?'

I was taken aback. And flattered. Not to mention tempted. Lord Hound of Tooting Bec had a ring to it. But I just couldn't do it.

'I'm sorry,' I said. 'I can't take it. Don't get me wrong. I really appreciate the gesture. And it would have been a huge honour. But it's Boris. Anyone who accepts an honour from him looks tainted. It makes you as bad as him . . .'

'Are you sure?' asked Dilyn. 'There are some total shockers in the Lords. Frosty the No Man. The son of a KGB spy. Michelle Mone . . .'

'Quite sure.'

'Then who can I give a peerage to? I don't know anyone else.'

I gave it some thought.

'How about Charlotte Owen?' I suggested.

'Who is she?'

'Just some junior Number 10 staffer.'

'Why her?'

'Because she opened the back door to the garden for us a couple of times. The whole point would be to pick someone no one has ever heard of. For no very obvious reason. It's a brilliant way of subverting the honours system.'

'Do you think she will accept?'

'Sure. She hasn't got anything better to do. She's only about eighteen. Probably on her gap year. It will be our in-joke. Only we will really know why she was chosen. People will be guessing for years to come.'

'Done. That's genius.'

'You will stay in touch, won't you?'

'Of course. Maybe you will come and stay sometime.'

'Maybe.'

There was a scratching sound. Larry was making another mark on the doorpost.

Chapter 14

This was getting to be habit forming. Cast your mind back to the Margaret Thatcher or Tony Blair eras. A dog could reasonably expect to live most of his life with just the one prime minister in Number 10. Now I was about to be on my fourth. I couldn't help thinking I might be getting a bit long in the tooth for it now.

'Don't,' said Pot Plant Two.

'Don't what?' I replied.

'Think about jacking it all in.'

'Why not? It's just revolving doors round here. I could have an easy life.'

'Sure. But now it's going to get interesting.'

'What do you mean?'

'Think about it. It's a straight choice between Rishi Sunak and Liz Truss. And Liz is going to win easily. Partly because Tory members are completely mad and partly because they haven't forgiven Rishi for helping to get rid of Boris. Left to their own devices, the Tory party would have Boris back in a heartbeat.'

'And . . .'

'And Liz is so obviously going to be a disaster. She will be a nightmare for the country but top-class entertainment for us. You can't give up a ringside seat. You'll dine out on this for years to come. It will guarantee you a slot on the after-dinner speech circuit.'

Pot Plant Two had a point. Maybe it would be fun to stick around if I could. After all, I'd had my eye on Liz for some years now. I had first met her during the EU referendum campaign when she had taken me to one side in the spin room at one of the debates and told me that Remain were going to win easily because deep down everyone knew that leaving would be deeply damaging to the economy. Since then, despite all the evidence to the contrary, Liz had managed to change her mind. Had reinvented herself as a poster girl for Brexit. She was the original tabula rasa. Conditioned to think whatever it was convenient to think in the moment. There was no past – no emotional or intellectual hinterland to Liz – only an ever-mutable present. Almost as if she was a 2-D cutout of herself.

What was it with all these people who had done politics, philosophy and economics at Oxford? Politicians are often moaning about worthless degree courses but the first one I would shut down is PPE. The damage it has done to the country is terrifying. Just a succession of inadequates pumped out into the world encouraged to think they can run the country. Both Liz and Rishi had done PPE, so we were going to be screwed whoever became the next leader of the Tory party. Whatever happened to a bit of impostor syndrome when you needed it? It would never occur to any of the dogs or humans I know to imagine that they might become prime minister. We'd be thinking of all the ways in which we might fail at the job. That's what I call a normal reaction. Healthy even. But not Liz or Rishi. They both felt they were born to do the job and would be brilliant at it. Mmm. We'll be the judge of that.

I guess that what convinced me to stay on in Number 10 for a while longer was Liz's launch event. This was the moment I fell in love with her a bit. Don't get me wrong, she was still obviously hopeless, but there was something endearing about her uselessness. It was as though she just couldn't see what was blindingly obvious to everyone but diehard Tory members. She was the perfect accident waiting to happen.

It was a gorgeous summer's day and I had bunked off from Number 10 to join a sizeable number of Tory MPs – Liz was already the clear favourite, so there were a lot of people hoping for ministerial positions in return for their obsequiousness – and lobby journalists in the offices of a financial services company in Westminster, where the Trusster was to kick-start her campaign. Her right-hand man and chancellor in waiting, Kwasi Kwarteng, introduced her. Skating over the flakier moments of her political career – i.e.

almost all of them – he declared, 'I give you Liz Truss, the next leader of the Tory party and the next prime minister.'

Nothing. Not a sign of Liz. Kwasi looked around anxiously. Perhaps she hadn't heard. After a while, he repeated himself. 'I give you Liz Truss, the next leader of the Tory party and the next prime minister.' Still nothing. Then there was a rattle on the door in the corner. Another rattle. It soon became clear that Liz was stuck behind it. Superb stuff. There were ripples of laughter from the press pack. Eventually, someone came to her rescue and let her in. It was a red-faced and flustered Liz who fought her way through the crowd to the stage.

Her speech was entirely forgettable. It was always thus. Public speaking was yet another thing to be added to the long list of things she wasn't very good at. Then a few questions from the media and it was all done. The Tory MPs all stood up to applaud her. Presumably for not falling over. At which point, Liz tried to leave. Only she had already forgotten the way out. She fought her way through the audience towards the back of the room.

Feeling a bit sorry for her, I felt I ought to intervene.

'Er, these are the windows,' I said. 'And we're on the first floor. I'm not sure this is the safest place for you to make an exit.'

'Oh,' she said, looking blank. She turned round to find a minder waiting to escort her back to the door.

Liz didn't seem particularly grateful to me for saving her life. Never mind. We had shared a moment. Just another small intervention of mine in the history of our country. Though I dare say not one mortgage holders would be thanking me for in a few months' time. But you do what you have to do. Liz and I would thereafter forever be inextricably linked.

The rest of the summer was fairly undemanding. As Liz and Rishi rushed around the country going from one pointless hustings and debate to another, precious little was happening in Downing Street. I would still go in each day but most days Boris was nowhere to be seen. He would hole up in the flat for hours on end, doing nothing. Occasionally, he would come down to his office, dressed only in his dressing gown and lucky underpants that had been given to him by Nadine Dorries, but even then, we tended not to speak. An uncompanionable silence.

This was most unlike him. Normally, he wittered on in his curiously syncopated voice – to amuse himself as much as the rest of us – but now he appeared to be broken. Lost in his own private misery. As if he was unable to process just what had happened to him. How a prime minister with the world at his feet could be reduced to a train wreck in just under three years. His self-absorption couldn't make sense of his downfall. It never occurred to him that he might have let himself and the country down with his lying. In his mind, it was the country that had betrayed him, not he the country. All he had ever wanted – all he had ever needed – was for people to love him. And now he was universally loathed. Held in contempt.

Nor could he be bothered to consider his legacy. To come up with one thing that might define his premiership other than Partygate. Largely because he had never imagined he might have to do something as prime minister. His imagination had never expanded beyond merely being prime minister. Getting to Number 10 had ever been the only goal. The summit of his ambition. So now he was to be left with almost nothing. He wouldn't be thanked for his handling of the Covid pandemic. He wouldn't be thanked for not having built any of the 40 new hospitals he had promised. He wouldn't be thanked for Brexit. If he was lucky, a few might remember him for his support for Ukraine. Not nothing. But not a lot.

Most days I would potter about in Number 10, answering a few emails each day and hanging out with Dilyn and Larry in my lunch hour. Nor was I especially lazy. Everyone was taking it easy. There wasn't a lot of point implementing a whole load of policies that would be cancelled by Liz when she became prime minister in September.

Then one day, I got a WhatsApp message from a number I didn't recognise. Could I please call this dog back? It was a matter of some urgency.

'Hi,' I said. 'This is Herbert Hound. You asked me to ring. Who am I speaking to please?'

'It's Muick,' a voice replied.

'Muick who?'

'I'm one of the queen's corgis. Sandy and I were wondering if you might be free to come to stay with us in Balmoral at the tail end of the summer?'

'Gosh. I see. I wasn't expecting this. May I ask why you are inviting me?'

'Of course. It's just that the queen always likes to fill the castle with family and friends at this time of year and she always encourages us to ask a guest as well. And you . . . we think you're interesting. There aren't many dogs who have worked in Number 10 for as long as you and we were impressed with the way you evacuated the dogs and cats out of Afghanistan. We wanted to meet you.'

'That's very kind,' I said. I could hardly contain my excitement. Off to stay with the queen. Things didn't get much better than that. 'I'd love to come.'

'Excellent. Don't forget to bring a basket. Balmoral isn't the most comfortable of castles.'

John and Jill were moderately pissed off that I now wouldn't be joining them on their trip to see Anna in the US, but even they had to concede that staying with the queen was too good an opportunity to pass up. So, a month later, I flew up to Aberdeen where there was a car waiting to take me to Balmoral.

My first impressions were that this was a rather dismal, forbidding place but I kept my thoughts to myself. Waiting by the front door were two corgis.

'You must be Muick and Sandy,' I said.

'Very nice to see you, Herbert.'

'Herbie.'

'Herbie.'

We did the traditional introductions of sniffing one another's bum before Muick led us indoors.

'Come and meet the queen. She's been dying to see you.'

I scratched my neck. Didn't want the queen getting a stray nit. Then followed the corgis into the living room where the queen was sitting on the sofa. Far smaller and frailer than I had expected.

'Herbie is here, Liz,' said Muick.

'Oh, splendid,' the queen replied. 'Come and sit next to me.'

'Thank you, your Majesty,' I said.

'Call me Liz. Nobody else does here apart from the dogs. You're amongst friends. Now, do you like smoked salmon? I have had some sandwiches specially prepared.'

'I love smoked salmon, Liz.'

'Oh good. I can see we are going to get on famously. Now come and tell me what's going on in Westminster. I want to hear all the latest gossip.'

We didn't stop talking for hours. I filled her in on Boris's attack of the glums and Liz Truss's ever more eccentric ideas and she told me about her own concerns for her family.

'Sometimes,' she sighed, 'it feels as if my dogs are the only things I can really trust round here. Now, if you don't mind, I'm feeling tired. So I'm going to have a lie-down before dinner. But feel free to explore wherever you want.'

The next few days were idyllic. More chats with the queen, walks on the moors with Charles and Camilla when they came to visit and quality time with Muick and Sandy. Considering their privileged upbringing, they were surprisingly down to earth. They wouldn't have looked out of place on Tooting Bec Common. Well, not that out of place. And the grub was sensational. I've never had such quality leftovers.

On the Monday, the queen invited us all to watch the Tory leadership announcement on the television. For the most part, we sat in silence.

'So, the Tory members have elected Liz Truss as expected,' she said.

'It appears so,' I replied non-committally.

'What do you think?'

'I think Liz Truss will be . . . very Liz Truss.'

'Quite. Enough said. Now she and Boris will be coming up tomorrow to do the official handover. Why don't you join me in the room? Curl up somewhere unobtrusive by the fire. I'm fed up with having to do all these ceremonial duties on my own. It will be good to have some company and share a laugh afterwards.'

I couldn't believe my ears. This was too good to be true.

'It would be an honour.'

Boris was the first to arrive on the following morning. I had worried that he might recognise me and wonder what I was doing there. But he was in the usual world of his own, where other people and dogs only existed as figments of his imagination. In any case, maybe I flattered myself. Maybe I had never made that much of an impression on him anyway.

'Good morning, prime minister,' said Liz.

'For the next half-hour,' growled Muick. I was beginning to warm to him.

It would be nice to say that Boris had made a bit of an effort. But he hadn't. His hair was still a total mess and his shirt was coming untucked. To be honest, he looked a wreck. He could barely talk in full sentences. It was the queen who had to do most of the talking. Boris merely gave one-word answers or muttered something about others bringing him down. No sense of responsibility for what had happened, even now. He seemed broken. As if the scale of his fall was only just sinking in. He was the man who had had the world handed to him on a plate and he had dropped it.

The queen looked towards the clock.

'You ought to leave now,' she said. 'Do try to take a break. Politics can be brutal.'

Boris nodded and waved an arm absent-mindedly. After a last handshake, he was gone.

'Christ,' said Liz, reaching for a drink. 'That was hard work. Thank God he's gone.'

'Look on the bright side,' said Sandy. 'At least you won't have to see him ever again.'

'There is that.'

Moments later, a member of staff knocked on the door. Liz Truss was here.

'Show her in,' said the queen.

Truss bounced in, all smiles.

'Isn't this great?' she said. 'Not sure about some of the furniture, mind.'

'Er . . . Yes. Congratulations. You are now formally prime minister.'

'I know I am! It's totally amazeballs. I'm called Liz and you're called Liz. It's almost as if it was written in the stars that I would become the next resident of Number 10.'

The queen tried to say something but couldn't get a word in edgeways.

'This is SO brilliant. I'm going to be the best prime minister ever,' said Truss. 'Just watch me. I'm going to cut taxes and get the country back on its feet in no time.'

'It might be an idea to take things a bit more slowly,' said the queen. 'Things have a nasty habit of unravelling if you go too fast.'

'No time like the present. I have some of the finest minds of their generation behind me. And the Institute of Economic Affairs.'

'Well, I won't interfere any more then.'

'Do you have any advice for me?'

'Just to shut the door behind you when you leave. It can get chilly.'

Truss made her exit. Twenty minutes of her had left me exhausted. God knows how the queen was feeling. She sighed. It was time for lunch. Later that afternoon, we were all taking a nap when Liz suddenly stirred.

'You know what?' she said. 'I think I might just have

had enough. I'm ninety-six and I'm getting far too old for all this. The sense of duty wears you down after a while. It's so bloody lonely being queen. Especially since Philip died. I've no one I can really talk to any more. I know that I have loyal courtiers but there's no one who has known me all my life. All my real friends are dead.

'My family are no real support. Charles is fairly useless. He means well but he's a bit dopey. And very prickly. Gets easily annoyed by the smallest things. Anne's OK, though she tends to keep herself to herself. Andrew is a total disaster area. If he's not begging me to fork out for his legal fees, he's pestering me for somewhere to live. He's never been the same since he stopped sweating. Have I forgotten someone?'

'Edward,' said Muick.

'Edward. Edward is Edward. Everyone forgets about him. Still, at least he's relatively harmless. William and Harry are at each other's throats about not very much. And now this. Liz Truss is the final straw. What's happened to my prime ministers these days? Winston was around when I came to the throne. Now, he was a proper politician. Even John Major wasn't so bad. But the recent ones have been a joke. Every time you think they can't get any worse, along comes another one to say, 'Hold my beer.' Think about it. David Cameron. Disaster. Theresa May. Disaster. Boris Johnson. Disaster. Now Liz Truss. Shaping up to be the worst of all. I just can't bear it any more. I don't want to be here to have to meet that Truss woman every week as she causes chaos. And I certainly don't want to be around for whoever succeeds her. So, you know what? I think it might be a good time to die. I've done my bit. Let Charles have a go. He's been desperate to be king for ages.'

Muick and Sandy just looked at one another. Not sure quite how to respond. So, it was left to me to say something.

'That all sounds totally fair enough,' I said. 'You've done more as queen than anyone could reasonably have expected. So, if you want to die, then that's completely OK. At the very least, you've earned the right to die at a time of your choosing. And I agree with you about Liz Truss. She's nuts.'

'Thank you, Herbie. I appreciate that. So many people seem to want me to live forever. It's a relief to be told I'm free to go.'

And Liz was as good as her word. Twenty-four hours later, she took to her bed and never left it. She died on the Thursday afternoon. I was allowed in with Muick and Sandy to say our goodbyes. She looked very peaceful. Almost happy.

Within hours, Balmoral was full of the entire royal family. Charles and Anne were there at the end, but not long after Andrew and William also arrived. Harry was the last to turn up, muttering something about having been snubbed. It was all a bit much. So many people obsessed with protocol and position. The grieving process seemed to be taking second place. I went to find Muick and Sandy, who were moping in the kitchen.

'I'm going to miss the queen so much,' said Muick.

'Me too,' Sandy agreed. 'She was very good to us. I loved her a lot.'

'And she loved you both very much,' I said.

'To make matters worse, we're going to be farmed out to Andrew,' said Muick. 'Can you imagine? Spending the rest of our lives with a self-obsessed sex maniac. We will be embarrassed to be seen out with him.'

There wasn't much to add to that. It was undeniably a bit shit. I put a paw round each of them and gave them a hug. Told them that I would always be there for them. That they were always welcome to stay with us in Tooting Bec and come to the Canines Anonymous meetings. With that, I packed up my basket and got a driver to take me back to the airport. This wasn't the moment to outstay my welcome.

Though that wasn't the last I heard from the two corgis. A week later, I got a WhatsApp from Muick. The queen had left instructions that she wanted me to join them both to keep a vigil over her coffin while she lay in state in Westminster Hall. It was one of my proudest moments to be slow-marched up the hall to take up my position by the queen for 30 minutes. I even managed not to wag my tail as the public filed past. It was the least I could do for a woman who had captured the country's respect and affection. She was loved by all of us. Even by Paddington Bear.

Once the funeral was over, the business of government quickly resumed. It was as if the ten days of mourning had been from a different era. A time when the nation had briefly come together in a common purpose. Now we were about to witness it falling apart again.

It would be wrong to say that I got to know Liz Truss well during her time in Number 10. I mean, how well can anyone really get to know someone in 49 days? But more than that, I'm not sure I would ever have felt any closer to her if she had remained in office for the next two years. Partly because Liz didn't even seem to know herself. Her self-image was totally at odds with reality. But there was also an absence in her soul. There was nothing of any substance to connect with. I can't imagine even a really good shrink managing to break down her defences. She was a walking personality disorder. Perfectly defended against reality. Which, come to think of it, seemed to be par for the course. Theresa May and Boris Johnson were just works in progress, readying us for the arrival of Liz Truss. It was as though the Tory party had spent the last six years punishing the country for its own pathology.

Not that Liz didn't make some effort to reach out to her staff. It's just that her communication skills were non-existent. On the day after the queen's funeral, she called us into an all-staff meeting. She wanted to lift morale by communicating her vision of the future.

'Hello everyone,' she bellowed. Liz only ever talked in a shouty voice, it seemed. 'I know that some of you will be feeling sad, but I want you to look on the bright side. The queen had a fantastic life and died happy in the knowledge that I was taking over as prime minister and that the country was in safe hands. She was at peace with herself when she died. She was ready to move on.

'And so are we. My government will put an end to the chaos of the May and Johnson era. We are ready for change, which is why the chancellor will be making sweeping changes in his upcoming mini budget. It's time for a Conservative government to introduce proper Conservative policies. Only then can we deliver the true Brexit bonus. Now, let's have three cheers for me. Hip hip . . .'

I'm not sure that anyone bothered to say hooray. This was more delusional than even I had imagined.

That afternoon I was sitting at my desk when Liz walked in, looking somewhat manic.

'I've got an important job for you,' she said.

'What is it?'

'I've neglected my Instagram account over the past few days. So, I need you to take some photos of me looking prime ministerial. To go with the ones of me in a tank. Let's go.'

So, for the next couple of hours, I followed Liz around Number 10. A photo of Liz standing next to the portrait of Margaret Thatcher. A photo of her sitting in the prime minister's seat at the table in the cabinet room. A photo of her in the garden. Some more intimate portraits of her in the Downing Street flat. That was the first time I had been able to have a proper snoop around the top floor. Christ, what a dump. The place was a tip. The gold wallpaper was peeling and the décor looked like it had been chosen by a five-year-old on acid. I don't know how Dilyn put up with it. I had a headache after just ten minutes.

'That's perfect,' said Liz as she went through the pictures on my phone. She spent the rest of the afternoon writing captions and uploading them to social media. 'A good politician always knows how to prioritise her time.'

'Quite,' I replied.

Well, we all know what happened next. A proper Conservative budget turned out to be a series of unfunded tax cuts and spending commitments. Largely because Liz had instructed Kwasi not to consult with the Bank of England or the Office for Budget Responsibility before dreaming up his imaginary figures. And the Brexit bonus proved to be the pound sinking against the dollar and a large increase in interest rates. Your mortgage has a long memory.

After that, things unravelled at speed. A disastrous Tory party conference at which Liz was forced to reverse the cut in the 45p rate of tax and then the sacking of the chancellor to try and save her credibility. Poor old Kwasi only found out he had been fired as he scrolled through Twitter on the way back from the US. Liz's legendary people skills to the fore again. That left Jeremy Hunt as the new chancellor. Not because he knew anything about economics – he knew less than me – but because he looked like someone who could pass for a chancellor. The last man standing in the gene puddle.

I, meanwhile, could only sit back and gawp. There was no work for me to do as everyone was in such a panic they took no notice of the dog. Not that there was much I could have done to reverse it. Nor would I have wanted to. No one could have planned a bigger shit show if they had tried. It was all I could do not to go into Downing Street each morning with a smile on my face. Larry was beside himself with excitement. He was about to outlast yet another prime minister. He even emailed the *Daily Star* to suggest they start a contest to see whether a lettuce could survive longer than Liz.

It could. Though Liz was in denial to the very end. Insistent that she had been forced out by malign establishment forces rather than through her own incompetence. If only she had been able to put more of her policies in place, then everything would have been fine, she said. What the country needed was More Liz not Less Liz. The country appeared to disagree. Still, it was hard not to feel sorry for her husband and her daughters, who were made to stand outside Number 10 as she gave her farewell speech as prime minister. They were the ones who would never hear the end of it.

There was just time for Liz to say goodbye to her staff. Though her heart wasn't in it. She was only just waking up to the humiliation.

'Look on the bright side,' said Pot Plant Two to Liz. 'At least you will now always be allowed to attend the

Cenotaph service on Remembrance Day. Just think. In twenty years, everyone will be asking themselves who that strange woman is standing next to the other former prime ministers. You'll be gone but not forgotten.'

'Wrong time,' I growled. 'Shut it.'

Then an embarrassed silence as Liz left the room.

Larry was snoozing by the front door. Waiting for his moment.

Chapter 15

That was it for me. Enough was enough. Tempting as it was to see if I could blag my way to another spell inside Number 10, my heart just wasn't in it. I couldn't deny the last seven years hadn't had their moments for someone fascinated by watching the political class in meltdown. But too much of that and the toxicity rubs off on you. Rather than feeling exhilarated by the proximity to power, I was now beginning to feel grubby. Like most dogs – XL bullies excepted – I wanted to feel useful and now it was getting increasingly hard to look myself in the mirror. Yes, along with Dilyn I had broken the Partygate story. Yes, I had brought back a plane full of dogs and cats from Afghanistan. But most people in the country were feeling worse about themselves now than they did when I started. Not a great legacy.

There was always the feeling that maybe the next time I could make a difference. Just give it one more go. But that was delusional. It seemed obvious to me that the Tories were going nowhere. Just marking time till the next election. Out of time and out of road. They didn't know if they were coming or going. After Liz Truss resigned, there was another leadership election in which the Conservatives had been nearly mad enough to vote Boris Johnson back in. The man whom they had booted out a few months earlier for being unfit to be prime minister. Imagine. So, instead, they chose Rishi Sunak whom they had previously rejected in favour of Liz. We were down to sloppy seconds. Soon anyone would be able to have a go.

Not that there was any chance of me staying on in Number 10, even if I had been so inclined. The new Team Rishi was a sharp-elbowed bunch of young men and women, hand-picked for their loyalty. Friends of Rishi. Friends of friends of Rishi. All of whom oozed the same sense of entitlement, believing that they were there on merit. That they were the ones with the answers to the country's problems. Despite all the evidence to the contrary. There would be no room for a dog in the new regime. I hadn't gone to the right school or university. I hadn't drunk the Kool Aid.

Nor did I warm to Rishi's dog, Nova. A fox-red retriever labrador cross. Maybe it was the age difference. She was only a couple of years old and very territorial. Everything revolved around her. All she could talk about was how she and Rishi liked to fast for thirty-six hours from Sunday night to Tuesday morning. How she and Rishi had a sweet tooth. I half expected her to say she binged on Haribos. She certainly didn't like other dogs much. Dilyn had warned me about her when she first arrived in Downing Street while Rishi was chancellor. A bit of an airhead was one of his kinder comments. She certainly didn't like me. Always barked down to me, even when it was clear she didn't know what she was saying. So we were never going to be kindred spirits. So much for the fellowship of dogs.

I didn't tell anyone what I was doing, as I didn't think anyone would notice when I was gone. First thing was to go and say my goodbyes.

'I'm off now,' I said to Larry.

'Don't leave me,' he replied.

'I've got to. It's the right time.'

'But you're the only thing that makes this place tolerable.'

'I feel the same way about you, Larry. We've had some good times. But I've had enough. I'm getting too old for this now. I'm over eleven. Most humans are long since retired at my age.'

'Tell me about it. I'll miss you.'

'And I'll miss you. You're the only cat I've ever liked.'

'You're not bad for a dog either.'

We embraced. Fur on fur. It was a tender moment and neither of us wanted to pull away.

'Stay in touch,' I said. 'You have my number.'

'You, too. It might be a couple of years off but come to an election-night party here. We'll have the place almost to ourselves.'

'That's a deal.'

I was just on the way out of my office when I heard a plaintive sigh. It was Pot Plant Two.

'What about me?' he quavered. 'You can't leave me here. None of the new crowd will pay me any attention. They won't even water me. They talk about governing with integrity, professionalism and accountability but they are happy to let me die.'

He had a point. 'OK,' I replied. 'How about I take you home with me? Do you fancy coming to live with us in Tooting? It's not quite as grand as your current situation and you will miss out on all the gossip, but you will be taken care of.'

'That would be amazing. And I'm sure I won't get bored. I might even start writing my autobiography. The things I've seen . . .'

I picked up Pot Plant Two, put him inside my rucksack and headed off to the Tube. Less than an hour later we were back in SW17.

'You're right,' said Pot Plant Two. 'The house is a bit pokey. But the front garden's nice and it's better than being left to die.'

Sometimes, he's all charm.

John and Jill were there to greet us and had no hesitation in making Pot Plant Two feel welcome.

'Where would you like to be?' asked Jill. 'Perhaps near the window so you can watch people come and go outside?'

Pot Plant Two looked around the room. 'If it's all the same,' he said, 'I'd like to be on the living-room table. That way I can watch the TV and keep up with what's going on in Westminster.'

'That's fine. Let me get you a glass of water.'

The two cats weren't quite so pleased to have me back in the house full time. I had hoped that my absence might have softened them, but quite the reverse. They continued to make my life miserable. Hissing out of the corners of their mouths, drinking out of my water bowl and blocking the stairs to prevent me having a lie-down on the bed. It was almost as if this was their only pleasure in life. I did once try to tell them about Larry, that things didn't need to be this way, but they just blanked me.

Readjusting to a life of doing not very much proved harder than expected. I'd wake up each morning with a sense of emptiness. A feeling that the whole day stretched out ahead of me with nothing to fill it. Everything felt a bit pointless and I struggled to find a routine. I even felt disengaged from my Canines Anonymous meetings, going more out of habit than a sense of purpose.

Even my efforts to regain fitness – I couldn't help feeling I had let myself go rather in Westminster – hit the skids. Out chasing a stick one morning, I could feel something go in my left back leg. A sharp stabbing pain. I limped back home and John took me to the vet. After a brief examination, the quack said that I had torn a cruciate ligament.

'He will need an operation,' he said. 'And it will be three months' rehab, part of it in a crate.'

No way was any of that happening. Least of all the crate bit. So, when we got home, I told Jill and John there was no way I was having the op. I'd do my own rehab and heal myself. Which I did. The injury seemed to give me the sense of purpose I had been lacking. I started off with short walks, then increasingly longer ones. Within a few months, I was walking without a limp. And I had saved John and Jill a £4K vet bill. Not that they ever thanked me.

Gradually, though, I fell into a routine. Get up early to look out at the back garden. John used to think I was just staring blankly into space but that's because he doesn't observe things properly. I know each and every plant in that garden. I can tell when each plant is about to flower. When I'm let out, I patrol the area and can smell the stray cats and foxes who have visited during the night. This is my domain.

Then off for a walk before watching TV with Pot Plant Two. Mainly the news channels, though we both enjoyed watching the football or cricket if it was on. Neither of us became addicted to the ongoing psychodrama of the Tory party. We just wanted to know how the death throes were going to play out. Pot Plant Two couldn't stop laughing when Rishi announced his five promises.

'The man is a halfwit,' he cackled. 'I've never seen a politician so bad at politics. How many of those promises do you think he's going to keep?'

'I dunno,' I said. 'Two? Maybe three?'

'One at most. Inflation will come down because that's out of his control anyway. Though he will try and take the credit. But he doesn't stand a prayer on debt, growth, stopping the small boats or hospital waiting lists. So, he's effectively just announced that he's failed. It's like he wants to lose the next election. Perhaps he's a Labour plant.'

Talking of which, I did get a message from Keir Starmer in the summer of 2023. Did I fancy joining his team as an adviser? I can't deny that I was tempted. Enough for me to go back in for a meeting at his office in Westminster. The spirit was willing. It was exciting to think that I might live long enough to actually see in a Labour government. Flattering to be asked to be a part in making it happen. But I needed to be realistic. I was now too old for what would effectively be a year-long election campaign.

'You're going to win anyway,' I told Keir. 'You don't need me.'

'I don't feel that confident,' he replied.

'I'm sure you don't. You're bound to be anxious. But trust me. The country is fed up. Everyone feels worse off than they were fourteen years ago. Almost nothing works as well as it did under Labour in 2010. Just keep reminding everyone about Partygate and Liz Truss. Tell them that their mortgage hasn't forgotten the mini budget, even if they are hazy on the details. You're going to be great. Hammer home the message that the Tories have wrecked everything. Though do also try to offer some hope.'

'It's been great talking to you. And I don't blame you for not wanting to become part of the team. It is all-consuming and you've earned a break. But it would be great if I could call you to pick your brains from time to time. Someone who knows the political system inside out.'

'Sure. Any time.'

'Just one more thing. Our slogan. What do you think it should be?'

'Simple. Change. It's time for change. Nobody can argue with that. Rishi will try to pretend that he is somehow nothing to do with any of the previous four Tory prime ministers but it won't work. He's part of the problem.'

'Thanks, Herbie. I appreciate that.'

I wasn't the only one feeling my age a bit. Within months, John had a major health scare and I was glad to be around. It was a Friday night – Jill was out doing ceramics – and John had just returned from the gym. He was looking extremely pale.

'What's up?' I asked.

'I'm not sure,' he said. 'I feel weird. I had a funny turn after coming off the cross-trainer. Light-headed. Almost out of body. A tightness in the chest. A pain in my left arm. I think I might have had a heart attack . . .'

'You think? It sounds like that's exactly what happened. So why are you still here and not at the hospital?'

'I'm not sure. I feel a bit better now. I wondered if I had maybe imagined the whole thing . . .'

'Maybe you have. But you can't afford to take chances. You need to get yourself checked out.'

'You're right.'

Just then Jill returned. She said much the same as me. Though not quite as politely. Within minutes they were on their way out the door.

'Don't die on me, John,' I said, as they left.

'I'll try not to,' he replied.

I was left all alone for the rest of the night. No fun. I was scared. Not knowing if I was ever going to see John again. A wake-up call for me. I was used to dogs dying. Only recently one of my best friends, Frida, had died. She was a good age. Fifteen. But it had been a shock, nonetheless. One week she had appeared fine, the next she was gone. Nice for her, I suppose. Though I would have preferred some time to say goodbye. It had never occurred to me that one of my humans might die before me. Against the natural order of things.

Eventually, Jill got home from the hospital. She tried to reassure me. The doctors thought John was going to be OK but they needed to make further investigations. It wasn't until five days later that John was allowed out. He had had a heart attack and an angioplasty had fixed a blockage in one of his coronary arteries. We both did a lot of sleeping in the following days. Along with a daily walk, of course. The shock had taken its toll on all of us. Even Pot Plant Two was vaguely sympathetic for a while. Unheard of. We all made John promise not to put us through that again. Try to exercise sensibly. You're not in your forties.

John wasn't the only person back from the dead. Much to my surprise, I got a video Facetime call from David Cameron. I hadn't heard a word from him since I had failed to turn up to the launch of his desperately dull political memoirs some years back. I just couldn't face all the self-serving lies and self-congratulatory speeches. Mind you, I could have done with the advance. Dave got the best part of £800K. A lot, lot more than I am getting for my own autobiography. And my book is far more accurate.

'Hi, Big Dave,' I said.

'It's now Lord Dave,' he replied. He couldn't keep the smirk off his face. A face that was weirdly unchanged despite the intervening six years. *The Picture of Dorian Gray*. Somewhere in his attic, there must be a portrait ageing by the hour. It was remarkable. Most former prime ministers look ravaged by the strain of office. But Dave is completely unaffected. No one ever found it easier to forgive himself for his mistakes than Dave.

'Hi, Lord Big Dave,' I corrected myself. 'What's with the peerage?'

'Isn't it great? Rishi has looked around all his Tory MPs and concluded none of them are any good. So he's asked me to be his foreign secretary.'

'That's mad. But you don't know anything about foreign policy. Last heard, you were responsible for Brexit. Not exactly a triumph of international diplomacy. And then you destabilised Libya by bombing it.'

'Details, Herbie. Details. These days, all a foreign secretary has to do is jet around the world first-class while trying not to start a war. It's a piece of piss. If James Cleverly could manage it, then anyone can.'

It was hard to fault his logic.

'So, I'm asking you if you fancy becoming my adviser in the foreign office,' he continued. 'You always were about the only vaguely competent member of my Number 10 Brexit team. And it won't be for very long. The Tories will be out of government soon enough. What do you say?'

'Er, thanks but no thanks. I've got my reputation to think of. But very kind of you to offer.'

'I thought you might say that. Never mind. Hope to see you again before too long.'

It always was easy come, easy go with Cameron.

Turning down new jobs was getting to be a habit. Still, it was reassuring to know I was missed and that I was still in demand. The glass ceiling for dogs had been well and truly broken. But there was one invitation I couldn't refuse. This one came through the post. A request – make that a summons – to give evidence before the Covid inquiry. As one of those who had been working inside Number 10 at the time, my presence was required.

The makeshift courtroom in Paddington was packed well before the start. It was as if no one had ever seen a dog on the witness stand before. Enough to make me feel nervous. Normally, I take these sorts of occasions in my stride. Dame Heather Hallett took her chair and we were off.

'I swear by Almighty Dog that the evidence I shall give is the truth, the whole truth and nothing but the truth.'

It was Hugo Keith asking the questions. Had all my WhatsApp messages been deleted like everyone else's? Er . . . no. As far as I was aware they were all still on my phone. Why wouldn't they be? Now it was Hugo's turn to look confused. Because everyone else had said some of their messages had mysteriously self-destructed. Clearly, no one had thought to remove any incriminating messages from the dog's phone.

We moved on. How was my memory of events in Downing Street during the pandemic? About as good as could be expected given the ongoing chaos. Trying to get Boris to concentrate on the data while stepping over one or two staffers who had been partying a bit too hard the night before. Trying to make myself heard above the karaoke machine while Michael Gove was asking Michelle Mone what had happened to the PPE she had promised to provide. There were a few gasps from the public gallery.

'I see,' said Hugo. 'That's all the questions I have for now. I suggest this is a good time to adjourn for a break.'

And that was that. My truth. Which didn't appear to be totally the same as everyone else's truth. Still, this wasn't my problem. The inquiry could make of it what they liked. They could ignore it or recall some of the earlier witnesses who had spent hours trying to apportion blame away from themselves. But this wasn't my fight. I could look myself in the mirror and feel good about myself. Boris, Dom and the rest could sweat it out. Not that there would be a real reckoning. People like them are rarely personally held to account.

We're getting to the end now. The death rattle of the Tory party was loud enough for even its devotees to hear by now. It was no longer a matter of if the Conservatives fell apart but when. The infighting became even fiercer and there were at least five different factions on the right all falling out with one another. The centre of the party had long since given up. They were entirely mute. Meanwhile Rishi got tetchier and tetchier as things collapsed around him. He couldn't understand why the country wasn't more grateful for all he had done for it. He even made the schoolboy error of getting his wife to introduce him at his final party conference. Nothing shouts 'I don't have a personality of my own' more than that.

Rishi joined his wife on stage to awkward applause once she had finished her five-minute speech. 'Marrying you is the best decision I ever made,' he declared. At which point I thought, 'If I had married the daughter of a billionaire, it would probably be one of the best decisions I ever made also.' Certainly up in the top three.

The final death knell came with the rattle of my phone. It was Larry.

'Long time no speak,' I said. 'Good to hear from you. What's up?'

'How are you Herbie?' he replied. He sounded breathless.

'I'm good.'

'Excellent. Now, the reason I'm calling you is because Rishi is going to call an election tomorrow for July the fourth.'

'How do you know?'

'I overheard Craig Williams saying he was about to put a bet on.'

'Who is Craig Williams?'

'Rishi's parliamentary private secretary. He's with the prime minister the whole time. If anyone knows, it's him.'

'But why is he doing it now? It's madness.'

'He thinks that if he succeeds in wrong-footing his own party then he must also be wrong-footing the opposition.'

'That's great. Thank you.'

'Don't just thank me. Put a bet on yourself. I have. I've put on a grand at five to one. Once it's paid out, I'm off on safari to the Serengeti. I've always wanted to see some lions.'

'But that's illegal. Insider knowledge.'

'Sure, it is. But there have to be some perks of living here. You can't even go out for a piss without the photographers snapping away. And who is ever going to suspect a cat?'

'You're right. You'll be fine. But I'm still not going to do it.'

'Suit yourself. By the way, that invite to an election-night party is still open.'

'You're on.'

I may not have been up for a bet but I was up for passing on the news. I called Keir. The election was going to be called the next day, I said. So, start writing your speech. Book the battle buses. Reserve the prime advertising sites. Get your social-media team activated. This is your moment to get ahead of the game.

'Are you sure about this?' Keir asked.

'Absolutely. My source is impeccable.'

'I won't forget this. I promise.'

'There's also one other thing I might be able to help you with . . .'

'What's that?'

'The Euros. I'm friends with one of Gareth Southgate's dogs. He's a cockapoo like me. He's offered to get Gareth to make the England team play really badly in the qualifiers and the first knock-out game. That way, the Tories don't get any feelgood bounce from the football before the election. Then, once it's over and you're in Number 10, everything changes. He can guarantee a penalty shoot-out victory and a last-minute winner. A place in the final is nailed on.'

'Do that and I will love you for ever, Herbie,' said Keir. He sounded almost tearful.

'Count on it.'

You know the rest. Well, not quite all. I did have a small part to play in Rishi Sunak missing the D-Day commemorations. Lord Big Dave did text me to say he was a bit worried that the prime minister was going home early and that it would look bad. I texted back to say that no one would mind in the slightest. Everyone was totally fed up with the 100-year-old World War II veterans as it was. Always going on about the sacrifices they had made. It was time to let bygones be bygones. We were fed up with the war and being grateful.

'You're right,' said Lord Big Dave. 'I'll tell Rishi it's fine for him to leave them on the beaches and come home to do an interview with ITV.'

Cameron really is the most gullible man I've ever met. So sweet. Needless to say, my next call was to Keir. Rishi's not going to be in Normandy for the international celebrations. So, make sure you are. And book your photo opportunities with Joe Biden, Emmanuel Macron, Olaf Scholz and Volodymyr Zelenskiy. Make sure that you're the one who looks like the prime minister.'

'Gotcha,' said Keir. 'I owe you again.'

That wasn't the end of it. Three weeks into the campaign, I couldn't resist getting in touch with Buddy. The schnauzer whose house Pippa Crerar lives in. 'I've got another story for you,' I said. I told him all about the insider betting on the date of the election.

'That's fantastic,' he smiled. 'Great narrative. Corruption in an out-of-control Downing Street. The Tories only in it for themselves. Pippa will have a field day with this.'

And she did. Poor old Rishi must have wondered why he could never seem to catch a break. But it was his election and his campaign. There wasn't a huge amount of affection for Labour but the country was agreed on one thing. They had had enough of the Tories.

Even so, I couldn't help feeling nervous as I made my way into an eerily empty Downing Street on the evening of 4 July to watch the results with Larry. What if all the polls that had consistently given Labour a twenty-point lead for the last six months were wrong? What if all those undecideds had chosen to give the Tories another chance? Because, well, the Tories are the natural party of government and people didn't really trust Starmer? What if my life was just one sick joke and I was doomed never to see a Labour government?

Larry and I held each other's paws as the clock moved round to 10 pm. Then the exit poll. Boom! Labour on course for a landslide victory. On a par with 1997.

'Tony Blair's not going to like this,' I said.

'Who's Tony Blair?' asked Larry.

There are some surprising gaps in Larry's knowledge. He thinks the world didn't exist before he was born. He's an expert on the five – shortly to be six – prime ministers he's known personally. But hopeless on the ones before that. I guess that's the difference between a dog and a cat for you.

'Tony Blair,' I said. 'The last Labour prime minister to get elected before Keir. He thinks only he is entitled to a landslide win. He's got a bit of a Messiah complex. Doesn't like any competition.'

'Oh.'

We stayed up throughout the night. Partly to see the exit poll, which we still couldn't quite trust, come true. Mainly to watch various former Tory ministers fail to get re-elected. There were cheers when Therese Coffey and Grant Shapps lost their seats. And Larry went wild when Liz Truss bit the dust. He had never liked her. Felt she was rude and disrespected him. However, we were both quite pleased when Jeremy Hunt held on. I mean, obviously he was a useless chancellor, but he was unfailingly polite.

Come early the next morning, Downing Street was beginning to fill up with the world's media. There to witness the change of government.

'You can stay to watch Rishi's farewell and Keir's arrival, if you like,' said Larry. 'It's history.'

But I was tired. Not used to this level of sleep deprivation. Besides, I would see and hear it all much better on the TV.

'I'm going to make a move,' I said. 'And you're going to have to get used to a new cat.'

'What?'

'The Starmers have a cat. Jojo.'

Larry didn't seem best pleased. Dogs he could tolerate. Not cats.

'Well, she'd better do as she's told. I'm the boss round here.'

'I'm sure she will be well behaved,' I said, trying to be reassuring. 'Even Keir knows you're the one really running the country.'

'Good.'

He went off to sharpen his claws for the ritual signing of the doorpost. Time for me to make my exit.

Chapter 16

Surely you didn't expect a happy ending? To the football, I mean. Gareth Southgate's dog may have been able to get England to the final of the Euros but he's not a miracle worker. Come the day of the match, the team reverted to type, passing sideways and slowly, and rarely looking threatening. Almost as if they were trying to make sure they didn't lose by too much from the start. Their equaliser took everyone by surprise. Spain's winner took no one by surprise. They were comfortably the better team.

So, no bragging rights or feel-good factor for Keir Starmer. Still, he had won the election so he couldn't be too greedy. For me, it was just a routine disappointment. A bit like watching Spurs. I'm not sure how I would cope if I was supporting a team that actually won anything. It would require a completely different mindset.

Imagine being John. Nine years old in 1966 and he thinks England wins every time. The last sixty-odd

years have been spent having that idea hammered out of him. In any case, this may well have been my last major international football tournament. Who knows if I will still be around for the World Cup in the USA, Canada and Mexico in two years' time? I will be nearly fifteen then. Over one hundred in human years. Not impossible. But unlikely. J. Alfred Prufrock measured his life out in coffee spoons. I've measured mine out in football tournaments. And prime ministers.

But then no one can really guarantee anything. You make plans based on what you hope is going to happen. For some of us, life then gets in the way. Bad things happen to good people. Some get ill. Some die. There is no rhyme or reason to it. If we're lucky, we get a wake-up call. John didn't even know he had a problem before his heart attack. That could have ended very differently. I don't say this to bring you down. It's just that the older you get, the more death concentrates the mind. No one has yet managed to beat the system. It will come for us all. The trick is to learn to live well first. To have as few regrets as possible.

So, these days I try to live by the Canines Anonymous mantra of 'one day at a time'. Obviously, it goes without saying, I'm not very good at it. I frequently get ahead of myself. We all do. I'm a dog after all. But I can say that I am, by and large, happier than I've ever been. I may be old, I may be tired, I may be creaky and I may not have many more years to live but I am content. I love Jill and John and I know that they love me. We have our routines. We suit each other perfectly. Even if they can get a bit needy at times. I really am too old to sit on their laps now. Cuddling up alongside them on the bed is more than enough for me.

I also have my friends. The dogs I go walking with on Tooting Common. The dogs I have met over the course of my career. We all keep in touch via WhatsApp these days. My needs are simple. As are my desires. All I really want is to leave the world a bit better than I found it. This isn't about what I have achieved in politics. God knows, I've been on the losing side enough times and it feels good to have ended on a high with a Labour government. But it's for others to judge these things.

All I know is that I've done my best. And had a few laughs along the way. Most of all, I would like to think I have left behind more love than there was before I was born. That dogs and humans feel better for my having existed. I certainly feel that way about them. That we have added, in a small way, to global happiness.

So, what now? Well, not much, I hope. Just walkies, naps and lots of cuddles. Plus watching daytime TV with Pot Plant Two. You wouldn't believe how much he has mellowed. He's now almost affectionate with us. He enjoys his life on the living-room table.

Now, it's time for other dogs to step up and take their place in government. Keir is going to need all the help he can get. His honeymoon period will only last a few months. He still rings me for my advice from time to time, but I'm now out of the loop. So we mainly talk about the football instead.

But life continues to have its surprises. A few weeks ago, I got a call from Muick.

'How would you feel about being made a knight?' he asked. 'I think you've earned it.'

'You know how I feel about the honours system, Muick,' I replied. 'I turned down the peerage from Dilyn, so I can't accept this one.'

'This one's different. It's not from Keir or any other politician. This one comes directly from the king.'

'What?'

'It's true. Charles admires you greatly. As did his mother. I know you only met the queen for a short while but you made a huge impression on her. She felt heard by you. Seen. You weren't just another courtier toadying to her or a family member asking for a favour. So please, reconsider, I beg you.'

'You've got to take it,' shouted Pot Plant Two. 'Just as long as you don't start pulling rank on me.'

'OK,' I said. 'I accept. It's an honour.'

So it was that a month or so later, Jill, John, Anna, Robbie and I drove down to Windsor Castle for my investiture. There to greet me were Muick and Sandy, along with Dilyn, Buddy, Pippin, Benny and several other of my dog friends. And not forgetting Larry. Though I'm not sure he enjoyed being an honorary dog for the day. Rather, he felt that we were all honorary cats. It was all very moving having them there. It was as if my whole life was there before me.

The king called me forward.

'How are your knees?' he enquired.

'Not so good,' I replied. 'But I can still just about manage to kneel.'

'Excellent. May I say what a privilege this is for me? My mother was a huge fan of yours. As am I.'

'Thank you, Your Majesty.'

I lowered my head as the king placed his sword on both my shoulders.

'Arise, Sir Herbert Hound.'

Acknowledgements

Every book I have written has been a team effort. This one more than most. The first thank-yous go to my editor, Andreas Campomar, at Constable and my agent, Matthew Hamilton, for believing in the book long before I did. This was not a book that came fully formed in the imagination. Rather it was an idea that emerged gradually from the central premise that my dog could have done a better job of governing the country over the last ten years. Thanks also to Holly Blood and Henry Lord at Little, Brown for caring so much about Herbert Hound.

Thanks also to my readers – Catherine Bennett, Anna Roads, John Sutherland, Richard English, Patrick Barkham, Jane Butcher and Tom and Debby Butler – for keeping me going throughout the writing process. Your input and suggestions have helped shaped the final version. And the title. Thank you for your time, creativity and affection for the dog.

As always, my friends and colleagues in Room 15 in Westminster have been a huge support. Telling me what's going on, making me laugh and generally keeping an eye on me. Thank you to Pippa Crerar, Jessica Elgot, Rowena Mason, Peter Walker, Andy Sparrow, Kiran Stacey, Eleni Courea, Aletha Adu, Ben Quinn, Rob Hutton, Maria Remle and Ellie Cole. Also to the editors at the *Guardian* for saving me from myself. Fay Schlesinger, Clare Margetson, Rebecca Allison and Frances Perraudin.

A heart attack wasn't what I had in mind in March 2024 when I was still in the early stages of writing. But Pitt Lim and all the staff in A&E and the cardiac unit at St George's Hospital in Tooting came to my rescue. I never did get to find out everyone's names, but you were all there for a total stranger when I needed you. I will never forget what you have done for me. Likewise to the mental health professionals who have just about kept the show on the road for more years than I can count. Thank you, Liz.

As always, huge thanks to my wife and soulmate, Jill, who has had to live with me and laugh in the right places during the writing process. A time when I invariably become a little more needy and clinically insane than usual. My children, Anna and Robbie, wisely left home years ago but are always in my thoughts.

Lastly, though, special thanks to Herbie for choosing to share his story with me. I had often wondered what he had been doing for the last ten years of his life. Now I know. It has been a privilege to share a home with him.